A Commonsense Approach to Dealing with People

A Commonsense Approach to Dealing with People

Managing People Made Easier

Terry "T. J." Jenkins

iUniverse, Inc.
Bloomington

A Commonsense Approach to Dealing with People
Managing People Made Easier

iUniverse books may be ordered through booksellers or by contacting:

iUniverse
1663 Liberty Drive
Bloomington, IN 47403
www.iuniverse.com
1-800-Authors (1-800-288-4677)

ISBN: 978-1-4620-1889-5(pbk)
ISBN: 978-1-4620-1891-8(clth)
ISBN: 978-1-4620-1890-1 (ebk)

Printed in the United States of America

iUniverse rev. date:06/28/2011

Acknowledgments

To my loving wife, Mary, for all your support for the past forty years. Your personal sacrifices and encouragement allowed me to gain the knowledge and experience that I'm about to share with you. Without her willingness to love and nurture our girls in my absence, I never could have achieved any success. Her commitments to the family made it possible for me to grow into the person I am today. To my girls—Dawn, Carrie, and Jennifer—who have shared the good and the bad that life has thrown at us. Together as a family, we have found that there is nothing that we couldn't work through. For those nights I worked and couldn't tuck them into bed, I know they understood why.

A special thanks to my longtime friend and mentor, Billy Ray Stevens. Thanks for teaching me the importance of patience and control in the chaotic world of information technology (IT). And to Jennifer Nemetz, a longtime friend and associate with great technical writing skills, who encouraged me to finish the book because she believed so much in my management style.

CONTENTS

Introduction

After more than twenty-seven years in the business of managing teams, it was obvious to me that people still struggle with dealing with people. I have been fortunate enough to have managed in the fast food, manufacturing, telecommunications, and the service industries during my career. Even without the word *manager* in your title, you manage people every day of your life. You manage expectations at work and at home with your family, friends, and business associates. There are probably thousands of people who manage people, and many of them may only have a high school education. I have been very fortunate during my career to have both positive and negative mentors along the way. I have seen what works well to motivate people and what things turn into demotivators. My mentors have been both college graduates and those who have worked their way up the ranks with just a high school diploma. Even though they may not have a higher education, some were very successful because of their use of common sense. Just imagine how successful you can be when combining both common sense and higher education.

I wanted to write a book that was easy to read and one that could also be used for a quick reference guide. I have put a picture of a toolbox at the end of each chapter with a takeaway tip under it. These tips are the main points from the chapter that I want you to add to your individual toolboxes. This way you will have a starting point when issues arise. After reading this book, I hope that managing people becomes a little easier for you.

Your tip will be here after each chapter.

Managing People Starts and Ends with You

Managing people is not as difficult as you may think it is. Using the commonsense approach, you already have some of the skills in your toolbox. When dealing with people, ask yourself these questions: How would I want to be treated in this situation? Do I like to be yelled at? Do I like being accused of being uncooperative? Do I like being talked down to? Of course, you don't. So why would anyone use this approach to manage people? There are those who would tell you that managing by intimidation gets results. I would suggest that you may get short-term results, but, in the long run, you will not have the respect of your team or keep them for any significant period of time. People do not like being made to feel that they are not important or that their opinion is not valued. They will take the first opportunity to find another job.

I had just started a new job and really wanted to impress my new boss. He called me into his office and asked me a question. I thought I knew the answer and gave him the details. He and his boss went to a meeting, and he needed to use the information that I had given him. Unfortunately for me, the information I gave him was incorrect. They both had their butts handed to them on a silver platter. Later that day, he called me into his office and closed the door. Without raising his voice, he told me the ground rules necessary for us to have a successful business relationship going forward. He said, "Son, when I ask you something, I need to know that the information you give me is accurate. It is okay to say, 'I don't know for sure, but let me check and get back to you.' I never want to have to eat crow as I did today because of wrong information. Are we clear?" And we were. I never forgot that lesson—and I still use it today when working with my teams.

Just as with any building, the foundation is the most important aspect of a good relationship. You can teach people the technical things, you can teach logic, and you can even teach them people skills. However, if you cannot trust someone, it is very difficult—if not impossible—to build a strong, lasting relationship. It is okay not to have all the answers—we just have to be upfront enough to admit it and then go find out the answers. I give everyone the benefit of the doubt. I believe that they are honest and want to do the right thing. No one wants to do a bad job. I will always assume that people are honest until proven otherwise. In the cutthroat world of business, you could say that someone with a trusting philosophy could be taken advantage of—and that could happen. However, there are many good people in this world; wouldn't it be a shame not to trust any of them? Just imagine all of the life experiences you could miss. You will learn quickly whom you can trust and whom you cannot. Would you want a promotion you gained at the expense of a coworker? Remember: you have to look at yourself in the mirror each morning—and you better like the person you see. Life is very short and fragile. If you do not enjoy life every day, it can pass you by quickly. Remember when you were in high school and someone who was thirty years old seemed really old? Then when you were in your thirties, people in their fifties seemed really old? Death was something that happened to old people—not us. Read the local newspaper and see how many times people have heart attacks in their forties and fifties. I lost a childhood friend at age nineteen and a brother at age twenty-seven. From that point on, I never missed an opportunity to tell family and friends that I loved them. My point is that we do not know how long we have on this earth—and we should take the time to enjoy ourselves. If you do not have balance in your life, it is very easy to be consumed with work. Someone once told me, "Life is what happens while you're planning." Do not let this happen to you. Do not miss the opportunity to see the kids' ball games or that dance recital. You will not regret it.

Managing people starts and ends with you. Recognize that you can positively affect or change your personal interactions with others.

Trust

The foundation of relationships starts with trust. Lack of knowledge, experience, or formal education can be corrected—as long as the relationship is based on trust. Do you want to work for or with someone you cannot trust? Not many people do. Trust is not a given. Trust is something that you have to earn one action or statement at a time. Trust is something that takes a long time to earn and can be lost in a second. A long time ago, my dad told me to tell the truth. It is much easier to remember the truth, he said. Once you start telling lies, it is harder to remember which story you told to whom. It is much easier to admit that you made a mistake, and deal with the fallout, than to start a web of deceit that continues to get more and more complex. Make no mistake: lying will catch up to you eventually. My dad quit school after third grade to start working in the coal mines to help provide food for his family. He worked there until his midtwenties when he started working at a brickyard. Although he did not have a lot of book learning, he was a very street-smart man. He could rebuild a motor—no matter what kind it was. He built his own permastone house from the ground up. He did all the masonry, plumbing, and electrical work on the house—and he maintained his normal job while doing it. During this process, he dealt with all kinds of people and companies with buying materials and tools. He never signed a contract in his life and really did not believe in them. He said his contract was his handshake and his word. His belief was that shaking someone's hand and giving your word was a commitment that you were going to keep. He said he did not need a contract to remind him of keeping his commitments. I have always believed that giving my word to someone was a binding agreement and that I was going to deliver what I committed.

How do you build trust in the workplace? If you are in charge of approving career planning or training for someone, make sure that you follow through on your commitment. When communicating, make sure that you have the facts before you communicate. People who communicate using incorrect information are faced with some major challenges to resolve. People may feel that you are attempting to either put one over on them (e.g., lying to them) or you are incompetent. Either way, it means a lot more work for you. Have you ever known someone who talks a good game, but comes up short when it is time to do something? Making and keeping commitments can help you build trust or destroy it. Do not make commitments to someone because it is what you think they want to hear. Make a commitment because you are going to make every attempt within your power to keep it. If you promise to call someone back by the end of the day with an answer, make sure you call back. Even if you do not have the answer, you promised to call them. Just put yourself in their shoes, "Did he or she forget about me? I must not be important enough to call back." Make the extra effort to call them back—even if it is only to say that you do not have the answer yet, but you did not forget them. Can you imagine the positive feeling that gives them? They are going to start to trust you, and you have just started to build the foundation of a new relationship.

I was working for a large conglomerate out of Detroit. We had several remote plants that provided products to the big three automakers. My boss received word that the local information technology (IT) person from one of the plants was resigning. He asked me to fly over and cover the operations until a replacement operator could be found. He estimated two to three weeks, but it ended up being six months. Even though it was longer than expected, it was a great experience. I not only was able to build relationships with the local folks, I was also able to see how not living in the corporate office could leave you feeling isolated. While I was at the remote location, the mainframe at corporate headquarters went down, and we were unable to process inventory or payroll. I was responsible for the data center back at headquarters and was used to being there whenever there was an issue with the systems. This time, I was at the a remote location and not able to see what was going on or have insight into how long it would take before we could start processing our data. I instituted a callback process where my operators called the thirteen remote locations every two hours with status updates. Even if there was no estimated time of arrival (ETA) on the systems coming back up, they called the locations with status updates to let them know that we had not forgotten them. That was the day I realized you need to consider both corporate and remote locations when putting together plans, communications, or policy.

Getting teams to trust each other can be a challenge. You have to set expectations on how the team members will interact with one another. When issues or personality conflicts occur, they need to be addressed as soon as possible. If you compare a negative attitude to a bad banana, you can see my point. A bad banana on a bunch of bananas will start to spoil the bunch. If you do not remove the bad banana (or conflict), it will affect your team's performance. The grocer's job is to keep the bananas fresh. Managers have the same responsibilities as the grocers. If you do not check on your teams daily, they can spoil. You need to communicate to them that you are all on the same team and are after the same results. If team members want to be viewed as professionals, then they need to act like professionals. You are their role model. If you project this trait, others will as well.

Trust: Set honest expectations and keep them; it can take years to earn trust—and seconds to lose it.

Honesty

You always have to be honest with people. It is too difficult to remember who you lied to. Even though you may not think it, people are watching you all the time. They see how you conduct yourself, how you act under pressure, and how you react to pressure. Do you deflect blame, or do you take responsibility for your team's results? Do not be one of those people who always fly off the handle. Get your facts straight before you make decisions or change things. Again, you are a role model for others, and you need to show it on a daily basis. Also, it is a small world and an even smaller business world. I run into people I worked with fifteen to twenty years ago. They remember you, and you remember them. An honest reputation far outweighs a liar's tarnished imaged.

My dad always told me to tell the truth. He said that once you start lying about things, you tend to make things up. Each time you tell a lie, it will change—and then you will have a hard time remembering to whom you told which version. It is always easier to tell the truth—even if it means taking your lumps for something you did wrong. You can deal with it, and you are done with it. When you lie about things, they can come back to bite you days, weeks, or years later.

In my travels today, I run into people I knew twenty or thirty years ago. We talk about the old days and the fun we had when we worked together. One thing will lead to another and, bam, there may be an opportunity for you or someone you know. There are always opportunities for honest, hardworking professionals who live their lives with honest values. It is surprising how old acquaintances can provide leads to future opportunities.

Have you ever found something that someone had lost? What did you do with it? I have found car keys, wallets, cell phones, and any number of other things in airports, rental cars, grocery stores, and malls. When I cannot find the owner, I will turn it in to the security department or the office. I know that some skeptics say the security people just take it home and will keep it instead of turning it in. This is where we get back to trusting the good intentions of others. I believe that most people are going to do the right thing; when lost items are turned in, they attempt to get them to their rightful owner. If there is a chance that I can get the item back to the rightful owner, I am going to take it. Lost and found is the first place I go if I lose something. We all know how it feels when you lose something—and getting it back can really brighten your day. Remember that being honest is doing what is right—even when no one is looking.

Honesty: Take the risk during a pressure situation to be honest—it is easier than trying to remember who you lied to.

Respect

Trust and honesty foster respect. Respect is not something that you can demand. It is something that is earned, one action and one conversation at a time. It is hard to regain trust once someone has been dishonest with you. At some time during our lives, we have all worked for people whom we have not respected. You remember the feeling—you did what was required and not much more. Most people will not go the extra mile for someone that they do not respect.

On the other hand, try to remember a time in your life where you really respected someone you worked for. You always wanted to do your best for them and not let them down. You did whatever it took to make sure that they were successful.

I remember changing jobs and taking over a new data center in Florida. I was coming from Michigan and was used to working in the corporate office. I wore three-piece suits and dress boots just about every day. The first week on the new job, we received about six pallets of paper for the data center printers. They came in after hours, and we had a limited number of operators to unload them. Not thinking anything about it, I started moving the boxes manually onto the computer room floor. By the time I was done with the last pallet, I needed a shower, but the operators had all the paper they needed to get through the night jobs. Years later, one of the operators told me he could not believe that I did that while wearing my vest and tie. He said that the previous manager would have never done that. I never asked any of my team to do anything that I would not do. From that day forward, all I had to do was keep their respect by walking the walk and talking the talk every day.

When you say one thing, but do the opposite, you are on the path to failure. Your actions show that you only care about yourself and not anyone else. It is walking the walk and talking the talk. You need to say what you mean and mean what you say. You cannot tell your people to do something one way and then do it another way. What kind of person would you want to work for?

Respect: Earn their respect—one person at a time. Treat everyone the way you would like to be treated.

Attitude

Your attitude is something that can make or break your ability to manage people. You may have heard the adages, "Is the glass half full or half empty?" or "You give me lemons and I'll find a way to make lemonade." These sayings hold true. Always look at things positively and do not assume the worst. I cannot believe that anyone would sit at home at night and dream up ways to mess things up at the office. Instead, it is usually a lack of training, insufficient skills, or a lack of direction that causes mistakes. On the other hand, it could also be that they are just not in the right job. When dealing with people, I prefer using honey instead of vinegar. Generations ago, parents used to give kids bad-tasting medicine using honey. Can you imagine attempting to get a kid to take medicine laced with vinegar? Yes, you are right—it would not be an easy task. If we compare this to an everyday work environment, we can see many similarities. When having to communicate a difficult issue, you are going to have a better chance of getting a positive result with honey instead of vinegar. This is where leaders put a positive spin on the situation and show how they can make it work. Some managers fall into a rut and say, "It is management's decision—not mine." They want to be their team members' friends and not their managers. They like delivering good news, but want to sidestep the difficult issues. Leaders will always find a positive way to explain things—and in a way that is respectful to the audience. When one door slams shut, another door opens!

I will knock myself out to help someone when they ask me something instead of telling me something. I am amazed by how many people today are afraid to use *please* and *thank you*. It is something most of us learned from our parents years ago. I include *please* and *thank you* in all of my e-mails and conversations. When someone asks me to do something, I will go to the ends of the earth to help accomplish the requests. When I am told to do something—rather than being asked with *please* or *thank you*—I feel as if I'm not appreciated or I am being talked down to. I will still get the request accomplished, but not with the spirit of teamwork that I do when I am asked politely.

As individuals and leaders, we choose every day to be positive or negative. Our attitude toward life and work will dictate our success. I want to work in an environment that fosters teamwork, fun, and a positive atmosphere. If I have to work every day, I want to be somewhere that I want to be—not some place that makes me unhappy.

A leader's attitude is contagious. Be a good leader; do not fall into the trap of discussing confidential issues or issues about people in the hallways and elevators. Discuss sensitive issues in private where no one can overhear you. When you see people discussing private or restricted conversations in nonprivate settings, it means that either they have lost sensitivity to their position or, even worse, they may have never had it.

If you are sincere and polite, people will respond positively. Try including *please* and *thank you* in every e-mail and conversation; you will see that it is not a hard concept. I am sure your parents added it to your personal toolbox years ago. I believe that one hand washes the other. You do not have to keep score, but when you are helpful to others, they will want to help you in return. Always try to be cooperative. It builds relationships and lets you know that people will be there to help when you need them. When people trust and respect you, they will go beyond their job responsibilities to help you be successful. Since not everyone can work in a good or great company, it is your job to make your company a great one. In some cases, it is best to take your ball and go play somewhere else (change companies). If that happens, never burn bridges. You and your reputation will be around for a long time. The business world is not as big as you think—and it is amazing how often people change companies. You may want to come back to your current company someday. If you leave under less-than-pleasant circumstances, you may not have that as an option. The short-term satisfaction of telling your boss off is not worth it. Instead, tap into your inner strength and be a better person than that; you are leaving to go someplace better. You may have heard the old saying, "Don't step on toes, as they may be attached to a butt you may have to kiss later." I have seen times where bosses and subordinates reverse their roles. That can make things very uncomfortable for both parties. Moreover, believe it or not, those bad times (and how you handled them) will be added to your toolbox. You can bet your bottom dollar that, in the future, you will not do the same things that caused you to leave your company. You just turned a negative into a positive. Good job!

Attitude: Take an opportunity to be helpful, and stay positive during a tough situation.

Making and Keeping Commitments

Have you ever waited at your house for someone to stop by to give you an estimate on a job you wanted done? Then they did not show up, and they did not have the courtesy to call you to let you know. How did that make you feel? If it happens more than once, I will not use them again. In this case, I was the customer and the no-show, no-call is totally unacceptable. As a customer, you have expectations that suppliers (lawn service, bug treatment, home repairs, new appliances, car repairs, etc.) must satisfy if they want to keep you as a customer.

Now put yourself in the role of the supplier, and someone has asked you for something. You always want to think before you commit yourself or your team. Damage to relationships can be done when commitments are missed. When your company's livelihood depends on those relationships, it is easy to see the importance of making and keeping commitments. You need to do everything within your power to keep commitments. Now for the real shocker—company team members are customers as well. They are internal customers and can be from other departments or even from within your own department. This is different from external customers that buy your products or services. Think of giving your commitment to an internal customer as a legally binding contract. Not that we need lawyers to get involved, but it is important enough to be concerned about the consequences of not meeting your customer's requests. If you know in advance that a deadline is in jeopardy, call your customer in advance and give them a heads-up. You don't call to say that you will not make it but just to let them know that you are running into challenges. Then commit to them that you will give them daily or weekly updates on the status until you are back on track. This builds trust between you and the customer. Nobody likes to get a call the day the project is due to find out that it's going to be late. Again, customers do not like surprises when it comes to their requests. Put yourself in your customer's shoes—wouldn't you want to know? The impact may be significant enough that they need to have an alternative plan in the event the project or job is late. This applies to the business world and your personal life as well. It does not matter if you are a customer, supplier, or the person doing the work; commitments are made and need to be kept. I am not aware of any statistical data, but from my personal experience, 90 percent of hostile customers come from missed commitments. Giving fair warning about missing a commitment at least keeps the customer in the loop—and it allows them to determine the next steps.

I remember a situation in the mid-eighties with a hardware vendor for a data center I was managing. They had a huge field failure on 3380 disk drives. We were losing three to four a week—and it was causing significant impact to our online systems. Since we were not the only customer in the area experiencing the issue, the local parts depot was running out of replacement disks frequently. I met with the account representative for the company and told him we needed to keep spares on site to minimize the downtime when we had failures. He said he would take care of it and would get back to me. A few days later, after not hearing from him, I left several messages for him. After no response, I went to the account representative's boss, and the boss said the account representative had never mentioned my request—and nobody was working on getting the spares on site. The account representative thought I would just go away and not check. He was no longer on the account after that. Keeping commitments builds trust—and it is impossible to have trust when someone is not honest with you.

Note: Never make commitments for other people. You would not want someone else making commitments for you—treat them the way you would want to be treated.

Making and keeping commitments: Set an expectation and, if unable to deliver, notify the requestor. If the commitment involves others, consult them before accepting commitments on their behalf.

Project a Positive Image

Smiling is a simple but effective way to project a positive image. No one likes to deal with a grumpy or mad person. It is an emotion that you have control over—even if you are not having the best day of your life. Smiling is contagious; you can give one away and get many in return. It is better than any stock market return, wouldn't you say? Say good morning, good afternoon, hello, hi, or ask them how they are doing today. People like dealing with someone that takes the time to ask about them (it is called caring). When you walk down the hall, do you keep your head up and greet people? When I pass someone looking downcast in the hall, several thoughts come to mind: they lack self-confidence; they are afraid to make eye contact; or maybe they are not happy. Being friendly is not hard, and it can be fun. Just imagine how many nice people you can meet and the experiences you can share. Life is short. Being positive can help you enjoy the trip.

I once worked for a director who was not well liked by his department. Everyone thought that he was mad at the world and could not be trusted. When he walked down the hall, he avoided eye contact and stared at the floor. I asked him about it one day. He said that he was not mad—he was usually thinking about the meeting he had just come from or the next meeting on his calendar. I told him that people assumed he was mad—and they made every attempt to avoid him. He was flabbergasted by what I told him. He slowly but surely started to acknowledge people in the hall. The morale of the department was positively changed. I also used to work with someone who did not like change. Every time his daily routine was changed for any reason, he would go nuts. It did not matter if it was a company policy, a department—or team-process change. He could come up with fifty reasons why it was dumb and why it would not work. He could never look at any change as being a good thing. It got so bad that no one wanted to work with him because he was always so negative. I attempted to mentor him, but he was not willing to change. After weeks of coaching him, I pulled him aside and said, "Life is too short to work in a job that makes you miserable. You need to find a job that makes you happy." A few weeks later, he left the company and changed his career field completely. He decided that turning his hobby into his job was the right thing to do for him. His entire attitude changed, and he was excited about working and life again. Sometimes we have to make difficult decisions about our careers. I believe that good things can happen to people when they have positive attitudes. That is why I choose to be positive and try to find the good in everything.

Project a positive image: Hold your head high and make eye contact with team members.

19

Treat Everyone the Same

The last time I checked, we all put our coats on the same way: one arm at a time. I have never felt that I was better than anyone else was. I believe that you should treat your subordinates, vice presidents, security guards, cafeteria workers, janitors, and peers the same. No matter what our social status, we are all human beings and deserve to be treated with dignity and respect. There is nothing wrong with us knowing the guard or janitor's name. What does this have to do with managing people? You should treat everyone from the top to the bottom of the organization the same. If you treat everyone as you would a customer—or your company's president—it is pretty easy to remember how to treat people. When you start treating people according to their social status, you are missing an opportunity to experience life. One Saturday afternoon, I was in a car dealership in the Midwest. A guy with a flannel shirt, jeans, and boots covered with manure walked in. The group of sales clerks saw him and immediately fled to the break room. One old salesman walked up to the customer, shook his hand, and asked if there was anything he could help him with. The farmer proceeded to pay cash for ten new trucks that he needed for his company. The sales clerks that assumed that he was not going to buy anything kicked themselves for missing out on the commission. The bottom line: do not judge people by their appearance or their job title. Those folks can have experiences in their toolboxes that you may not have. Sharing these experiences helps us add to our own toolbox. When we stop learning and adding to our toolbox, it may be time to retire.

There is an old adage, "Never judge a book by its cover." I am fortunate enough to have always been able to strike up a conversation with perfect strangers. Sometimes small talk can really get people to open up and share their life experiences. My wife and I were returning from a trip and were delayed in Dallas Airport for several hours. While sitting at the gate, a lady sat down across from us, carrying what appeared to be a large photo album. We started making small talk and learned that she was a volunteer on her way home from three months of supporting Hurricane Katrina victims. The photo album included pictures she had taken from her experience in the restoration of life to the Gulf Region. She shared her thoughts for more than an hour; my wife and I had a totally new respect for not only the victims, but also the volunteers who stopped their lives to help others. To see the pictures of the devastation and hear the positive spin she put on the experience was amazing.

During flights, I have sat next to the president of a company who refused to fly first class because his company would not let all team members fly first class. I sat next to an elderly gentleman who told stories of his war experiences and how they would do it again to save this country. We are all just trying to get through life and provide for our families. No matter what our status is in life, we all have experiences that positively affect others. Leaders embrace everyone and are willing to get to know people and gain from their experiences. Do not cheat yourself out of the many opportunities that present themselves every day.

Treat everyone the same: Engage folks in all levels of the company—regardless of their career position or social status.

Be Nice

When was the last time you heard that? Did your parents ever tell you that if you could not say something nice about someone, do not say anything at all? It is true. Believe it or not, people listen to—and believe—what you say. A team needs everyone pulling together for the common good of the department or company. If you set an example of talking behind someone's back, more than likely your team will do the same. Look for the good in everyone and everything. It takes a special toolbox to be able to look problems in the face and turn them into opportunities. Have you ever done something nice for someone without being asked to or expecting credit for doing it? I always look for ways to do nice things for people without being asked. In my last job, I traveled through airports approximately two weeks a month. Spending that much time in airports, you have many opportunities to spread kindness. I would look for a military person standing in line for food and would try to position myself behind them. When we would reach the cash register, I would tell the clerk to put his or her food on my bill. Sometimes it was just a drink or sometimes a meal, but the recipients' reactions were always the same. I would shake their hands and thank them for serving their country. It was one of the most rewarding feelings I had ever experienced in my life. Maybe it is because I am a veteran, or maybe it is because I was in the service during Vietnam and saw the way many of my comrades were treated when they returned home. I know the sacrifices these folks make, and if me buying them a cup of coffee or a sandwich puts a smile on their faces, it is worth every penny. Even if you do not travel, you can do it in your own office. Help a peer without them asking, buy them a cup of coffee at the cafeteria, or take them to lunch for no reason.Random acts of kindness are great ways to show people that someone cares. Try it—and see if you are not bitten by the kindness bug. Did you ever unexpectedly get a card or flowers from someone? Do you remember how it made you feel? When people get married, have a child, or experience a loss in their family, make an effort to let them know you care. What are you doing to set yourself apart from other managers or other companies? It is called caring about the people you work with, and there is nothing wrong with that.

I had a peer director who was over the department's finance group. She was always pleasant and helpful no matter when you called or sent her an e-mail. Her beliefs were that she was going to do anything and everything to help her customers be successful. Whenever there were budget issues, she was available to help you get the answers or solutions to the issue. When sensitive issues came up, she had a way of putting people in their place with a smile on her face. She never lost control, used inappropriate language, or played games with people. You always knew where you stood with her. She was the type of person who you not only liked working with but also would have loved to work for.

Be nice: Take the time to make an honest, sincere gesture—without expecting credit.

Just the Facts

A big part of being in control is making sure that you have all the facts before making changes or taking action. No one wants to look silly in the eyes of his or her customers, peers, or boss. How many times have you seen someone come up with an idea and send out an e-mail on a new process? Then, after they get feedback from someone, they send out another e-mail changing the previous e-mail. This drives me nuts and makes the sender look as if they did not put a lot of thought into the process. Part of being a good leader is to be able to lead by setting direction and communicating it correctly. Shooting from the hip with decision-making can be used when the circumstances dictate that approach, but I do not recommend it for the long term or as the preferred management style. Your team members have to trust you; they notice if you are organized, if you make good decisions, and if you communicate with them in a positive manner. They also need to know that you are big enough to admit that you may have made a mistake. Do not forget that you are human—and you will learn from your mistakes just as they do.

Some simple tips to help you be successful:

Before making changes, decisions, or taking corrective actions, get your facts straight.

Do not react emotionally or be drawn into an argument. Regroup instead.

Abandon ill-prepared responses. Offer to check into the matter and get back to them instead.

If someone asks you a question, it is okay to say, "I don't know, but I'll find out." Last time I checked, nobody had all the answers.

Tip: Never, ever respond immediately to an e-mail, voice mail, or situation that makes you mad. People who have a tendency to take things personally will often fire back to protect their good names and reputations. I believe that this is one of the worst things you can do. You need to take time to research the issue, get your facts together, and respond in a professional manner. Cooling down, seeking information, and putting together a response that will be professional (and not attacking the individual) will go a long way in getting the issue resolved.

Just the facts: Defuse an emotional situation and return team members to the facts of the situation. Use a cooling-down period.

27

Don't Make It Personal—Don't Take It Personally

Too many times, I have seen differences of opinion lead to personal attacks during meetings or in e-mails. It is okay to question a process or policy that you do not agree with or understand. How well you can present your questions will make the difference between being successful or failing. It's not what you say, but how you say it.

Never attack the person. If necessary, question the process. People take pride in building things, whether they are processes or products. When you ask why, it can be taken as a personal attack. This can lead to dissension within the team and has caused many projects to fail. A good way to ensure support is to include them in the discussion or the creation of a process or product. By getting their involvement from the beginning, they understand it, can question it, can accept it, and can be a part of the solution. People will accept change like this much better than getting something crammed down their throats.

Instead of saying, "This process stinks, what the heck were you thinking?"—a less threatening approach would be, "Can you help me understand how this process was built and what the purpose for it was?" Then listen carefully so that you understand the history behind it. A process is built at a specific point in time and is never intended to last a lifetime. As time goes on, the environments or circumstances surrounding the project can change. Just because we built a great process last year does not mean that you never have to revisit the process for improvements. Another approach that I like to use is to compliment the process and then ask if there is a way to make the process even better. This is not an attack on the person—and it is striving for perfection. It's hard for any process builder to be conceited enough to think that his or her process is perfect.

I worked for a company that had a great leader in its customer service division. One day we were talking about change and how it affects the people and the company. He told me that the mark of a great leader is to make a decision and communicate it well. He said it could take time to determine whether the decision was a good one or not. A leader will check on the performance of the decision periodically to determine whether the desired outcome is being achieved. If you are living with a decision you made two or three years ago—and it is still working—you can usually be comfortable that you made a good decision. He also mentioned that job hoppers really have difficulty in measuring success. So many times, executives jump from jobs every two or three years. By the time the executive leaves and someone new comes in and changes everything, it is almost impossible to determine the success of the previous leader. It is very difficult for teams, departments, and companies to gain and maintain momentum when executives roll in and out like a revolving door. It is almost like starting over each time, and valuable time and momentum are lost. The morale of the team and the company can be negatively impacted by this constant change in upper management. Many people want to stay at a company until they retire. I have always started each job in my career with the belief that I would retire there. It is kind of like playing poker and being all in. I will give 150 percent to my customers, my team, and the company until I leave that company.

Another thing that has always troubled me was the use of contractors in certain companies. It is also a shame when you have a good IT team at a company and a new executive comes in and does not get to know the team (and what the team has accomplished) before they start changing things.

I once worked for a company where a new chief information officer (CIO) came in and, for the first thirty days, he met with all the customers of IT in the company. During those thirty days, he never interviewed anyone in the IT department below the directors he brought in. In the second thirty days, he outsourced the entire data center team and programming staff. I believe that he failed as a leader. He never attempted to learn what IT had built or why the systems were the way they were. The manufacturing application had been bought by the customer without IT review and approval, and then the customer handed the application over to the IT group for support. It did not meet the customer's needs from day one and had to be modified for the next ten years to meet the customer's changing business needs. To me, a great leader would have done a discovery with the customers and the management of the IT team to get all of the facts before turning things upside down. Decisions should be made with all the facts and not just emotional feedback from customers. I believe that his limited view of the IT side of the environment limited his choices for improving the customer experience.

Under his leadership, we signed a two-year off-shoring contract for a new Order Entry System. Two years—and twenty million dollars—later, they pulled the plug on the project without delivering a finished product. He left the company shortly thereafter. He had in-house resources available that were capable of building the application in house, but he never even considered that as an option because of his feedback from the customers. Outsourcing part or all of IT teams and projects are viable solutions. Leaders need to make sure that they get all the facts when making major personnel and system decisions.

Don't make it personal—don't take it personally: Find flaws in the design, process, or tasks instead of the individuals—discourage personal attacks in meetings and e-mails.

Teaming

This is where we really test our maturity and professionalism. It is time to step back and not be concerned with me, me, me. We have to set our egos aside for the good of the team, department, and company. I would like you to think about this long and hard. When you are good at what you do, you do not have to try to impress people. They will respect you based on your actions and results. Building teams sometimes requires a manager to go out of his or her way to help the team be successful. You want teams to think for themselves—and you can coach them in that direction. There is no better feeling for a leader than to see a team grow and mature into a self-sustaining part of the department or company.

You cannot let previous cultures or barriers stand in your way. The bottom line is for your company to be successful in the long term. Communicating and building trust between departments can pay tremendous rewards to the company's success. It is time to stick that ego on the shelf and grow up. Companies are individuals working together to make a better team.

Teaming with local teams is considerably easier than with remote teams. I believe that it is people's nature to work better when they are face to face. You can get to know the folks better and actually see their reactions. Once you understand their emotions, you can help coach to improve their teaming skills. Supporting remote teams in different time zones becomes more of a challenge. A true leader will find a way to get to know his or her remote team members to help them grow as well. This can require scheduling more one-on-one meetings and video conference calls. Always try to be considerate when scheduling meetings, keeping in mind everyone's lunch breaks, start, and stop times. There is nothing worse than East Coast folks being invited to a 6:00 p.m. or 7:00 p.m. meeting. By the same token, a 9:00 a.m. meeting on the East Coast is 6:00 a.m. on the West Coast. Be considerate when scheduling both recurring and one-time meetings. I believe that you have to build strong relationships in both cases. Those relationships are built on trust and mutual respect. I like to compare being a great leader to being a farmer. You are always concerned with growing your team, just as a farmer is with getting the best yield from his or her crops. Sometimes you can select your own team, or you may have taken over an existing team. In either case, you want the team to grow and flourish to its fullest potential. As I mentioned earlier, you have great teams when individuals can put their personal agendas aside for the big picture or the good of the group.

Leaders must be able to communicate and sell their vision. Many times, you may see resistance when attempting to share your vision. A person's normal reaction is to resist change and, sometimes, it is all about the timing. It may be a great idea, but the time is just not right. Other times, it is too much information too fast for them to comprehend. This is where my belief of planting seeds comes in. Sometimes you are better off giving one or two possible solutions to an issue. Then just walk away and give people time to think about it. Not all people can think fast on their feet, and they may need time to think about the challenge in front of them. They like to replay it in their minds and come up with pros and cons. Once they have a chance to digest it, they will usually see what you are attempting to say or do. Many times, I have had people come back to me days or weeks later with solutions that are variations of the ideas I planted. The bottom line is that the team developed a better solution because the team was a part of the solution. It is more important to me that a good solution was found than for me to take credit for bringing it up.

Teaming: Set aside a personal preference or agenda for the good of the team.

Good Communication is Key to Managing People

Oral communication skills are always a challenge. People like to work within their comfort zones. Talking to someone you do not know very well—or in groups of people—terrifies many of us. Start with small groups and do it often. There are all kinds of self-help books and organizations (such as Toastmasters™) that will help you overcome this obstacle. Just remember that to be good at anything, you have to practice. Mark McGwire did not hit all those home runs without taking batting practice.

Nothing beats spending a few minutes talking face-to-face to build teams, relationships, and company spirit. I worked for a company that had one of the best leaders I have ever worked for in my career. It was a small company, and the leader would walk through the office one day a week. He would stop and talk to people at their desks or in the halls. He would ask how things were going, and you could tell he really cared about the staff members' input. Everyone knew him by sight and felt comfortable talking to him. He would always respond to e-mails once he had time to research the issue. If he did not respond by e-mail, he would mention the issue when he stopped by during his once-a-week walkthrough. Whenever there was a big announcement, he would schedule a meeting in the cafeteria and deliver it personally with his vice presidents (VPs) by his side. Everyone in the company got the same message—and the direction of the company was clear. He would take questions and never avoided the difficult ones (which people respected him for). Because of his management style and personality, he would tell you if he could not answer because the information was confidential, but you trusted him to have the team's best interest in mind.

Written communication has its challenges as well. It is always challenging to put together a letter or e-mail that can communicate what the author is attempting to say. How many times have you received an e-mail that lit a fire under your fanny? E-mail is the most misused tool in anyone's toolbox today. Use it for communicating information; do not use it to convince someone about one of your ideas or feelings. Never respond to an e-mail that has upset you without letting time pass. When you get an e-mail that upsets you, you have some choices to make. Do I fire back and let them have it? Do I pick up the phone and give them an earful? Emotions have a way of getting in the way of our goals. Deal with facts and not emotions—it will make life much easier.

Some reminders on e-mail communications:

Don't respond until you calm down.
Never attack the individual—address the issue.
If the e-mail is more than three threads long (been sent at least three times), pick up the phone and call the person. If you have not explained it in three attempts, you are probably not going to without talking to the individual.

Some of us prefer written or oral communication to the other; however, remember that well-rounded communication skills will make your toolbox more attractive for the next opportunity. Getting outside of your comfort zone can pay dividends later in life. Here are additional reminders to help you build your communications tool set.

Effective Communications:

- You can't learn something new by talking.
- Repeat what you thought you heard.
- Be sincere and caring.
- Be an active listener.
- Stay tuned to the speaker.
- Look the speaker in the eye.

Physical:

- Control your body language.
- Stop typing and turn away from that keyboard.
- Let the phone ring: your voice mail will talk to anyone.
- Written (reread for clarity and to ensure you are saying what you mean).
- Oral (speak clearly).
- Think about what you are saying before you open your mouth or put it in print.
- Visit team members (walk around daily or weekly).

Vary the Approach:

- Communicate using different approaches. After attempting to explain something multiple times, if they don't understand, consider that it could be you.
- What if they still do not get it?
- Have you tried a third party?
- Let them vent (do not interrupt).
- Listen closely to their side of the story.
- If they are physically upset, schedule a time for you to get back to them.
- Do not be confrontational or defensive.
- Be willing to give up something for the success of the team.
- Find a mediator, if necessary.

Good communications is key to managing people: Move outside of your comfort zone and speak to a small group or polish your writing skills.

Effective Listening

One of the biggest challenges for everyone is being a good listener. How many relationships have been ruined, business deals gone south, and companies failed because of poor communications? The answer is a lot. Apply the following commonsense rules to improve your listening skills significantly.

Learn by listening. You never learn something new by talking. How many times have you observed a conversation where neither party is willing to listen because they are more concerned with selling their feelings or agendas? Probably more times than you would like to remember. Remember that learning something new adds to your toolbox.

Repeat what you thought you heard. Do not walk away from a meeting or conversation without clarifying what each of you is going to do. Many hours, dollars, and careers are wasted because people were ready to start something before they totally understood what it was that they were really being asked to do.

Control your body language. Have you ever had a conversation with someone that you could tell did not want to be there? It is very hard to get excited about an idea or project when people are tuning you out. Look the person in the eye. Focus on what they are saying. Do not cross your arms, roll your eyes, slouch away from, or look everywhere except at the person speaking. There are many self-help books on body language that will give you a better understanding of the perceptions of body language.

Be sincere and caring. People know when others are insincere. It is as if everyone has a built-in sincerity detector at birth. It will take people about five minutes of conversation to judge whether your intentions are sincere. Some managers may tell you not to get too close to your people. There is a fine line between knowing your people and knowing too much, but I believe that true leaders can do it. People need to talk and know that their boss understands and cares about them. Taking time to know people will enrich your life tenfold. Again, when you are honest with yourself and others, the rest will take care of itself.

Be an active listener. Stay tuned into the speaker. Ask clarifying questions to ensure that you understand what they are saying. There is nothing wrong with asking someone to clarify or restate what he or she said. The bigger mistake is not understanding and not asking. We have all been programmed since first grade to laugh at someone when they ask a dumb question. It is understandable that most people do not want to be embarrassed in front of others. I feel that the only dumb question is the question that is not asked. How many times have you heard someone ask a question that you were thinking about, but you would not ask in front of the group? Active listeners will never shut down a brainstorming session. Leaders who do this not only kill the creativity and innovation, but also the passion of the team. When listening to someone, do not be afraid to look him or her straight in the eye. When you avoid eye contact, people may believe you are lying. All good relationships depend on trusting the other party or parties. How many people do you trust that will not look you in the eye?

Create the right environment. A leader will create a safe place for asking questions. A safe place is an environment where people feel comfortable speaking openly without fear of being teased or laughed at. I believe that not having a safe place will significantly limit your ability to foster creativity, teamwork, and passion within your team. Happy people will perform much better than those who are just going through the motions. What kind of team members do you want?

Keep multitasking in its place. A leader should give people his or her undivided attention. Leaders should not be listening to multiple conversations or working on their personal computers (PCs) or thinking of their next meeting. A good leader will *be here now.*

When a team respects its members, it will not make fun of someone for asking questions. Clarifying questions can save time and money and can determine the success of a project. Do not be afraid to ask questions.

Effective listening: Make eye contact. Don't interrupt—let the person speak. You cannot learn something if you are talking.

Timely Response

Have you ever felt the frustration of leaving a voice mail or e-mail for someone and not hearing back from him or her for days—or, even worse, not at all? It is possible for people to get one hundred to two hundred e-mails and twenty voice mails a day. Staying on top of e-mails and returning voice mail messages takes a huge commitment. It is important to understand that your level in the company will have a direct correlation to the volume of e-mail you could receive. The more people you support, the more project status updates or involvement the manager can be involved in. Managers will generally get more e-mail than individual contributors will because they get carbon copied on issues to their team members. And, by the same token, directors can receive more than managers. At my last company, it was normal for me to receive more than two hundred e-mails per day as a director.

Some e-mail tips I like to use:

- Only send TO: people you need a response from.
- Only send CC: people needing to be informed.
- Never send TO: or CC: someone's boss for leverage if the individual failed to respond to your request.
- Never send TO: or CC: just to cover your backside.

How many times have you seen someone spam an entire group, department, or a VP because they are frustrated that they cannot get a response from a peer? E-mail should never be used as a threat.

Set up some guidelines for e-mail etiquette:

- I will e-mail and then call before escalating an issue to someone's boss.
- I will only expect responses from the person or persons in the TO: line.
- I will not Respond All to an e-mail when I have concerns. Instead, I will contact the sender directly.
- I will not respond to ping-pong e-mails. For any e-mails with more than three strings, I will set up a meeting to discuss.
- For important issues, I will tag the subject line with:

  - Approval Required
  - Status Requested
  - Direction Requests

I will pick up the phone and call for emergencies or critical issues. I will not assume that the recipient is sitting in front of the computer and is able to respond immediately. I have a personal philosophy that says I will do the following with my e-mails:

- I will not go home with more than ten unread e-mails in my inbox.
- I will address the e-mails from the previous day before starting my next day's e-mails.
- I will acknowledge all e-mails within twenty-four hours (even if I do not have the final answer).
- Those issues that need addressing go to the top of my Things To Do Today list.

Guidelines similar to these will help the recipient know that you need a timely response. It is very frustrating not to get assistance when you ask for it. Leaders should be a part of the solution, not a part of the problem.

I once had a manager who was very poor at keeping up with e-mails. I would have to wait days or weeks for responses—and sometimes I would not get a response at all. This was very frustrating, and it severely limited my ability to work through issues and set direction in a timely manner. Over the years, I have seen people keep copies of every e-mail that they sent so that they could cover their backside. This is a poor work environment to work in—and it can be very detrimental to the organization. The amount of effort spent on looking over your shoulder could be more wisely spent on moving the organization forward. It not only delays actions but, after a while, it will give the perception that you—or your need for support—are not important. It destroys your morale, and, if left uncorrected, causes the company or team to lose good people. I do not believe that anyone enjoys going to work in an environment where they feel unwanted or unappreciated.

Some additional commonsense tips for e-mail:

- Update your e-mail's out-of-office reply tool when you are not available (even for long meetings).
- Update your voice mail mailbox message.
- When not available, let the requestor know when you will return, and whom to contact in your absence.
- Use the e-mail preview pane screen to quickly review e-mails that need immediate attention.
- Review and respond to new e-mails each morning before starting your daily routine.

Some common practices that make life easier:

- Do not send out a lengthy document and expect it to be reviewed and discussed in a meeting without giving the recipient forty-eight to seventy-two hours of lead time.
- Use voice mail for what it was intended. Leave a message requesting information, don't say call me. We all have been caught in the old voice mail tag game.

Each e-mail or voice mail deserves some type of response or action. A response—either positive or negative—is better than no response at all. Have you ever received voice mails from headhunters wanting to provide services to your company? Even if you are not interested, they will keep calling and calling. Take five minutes to call them back and let them know that you are not interested at this time. They can be quite persistent in leaving messages. You will probably spend more than five minutes listening to their messages and deleting them if you do not ask them to stop calling.

Timely response: Set voice mail and e-mail options for out of office or delayed response if in training or lengthy meetings with whom to contact while you are unavailable.

Helpful Hints

- Always ask people if this is a good time to speak with them. Just because they answered the phone doesn't mean that you have their attention.
- Respect their work time. It is very difficult to get things completed when you are constantly being interrupted. Schedule a meeting, if necessary, or cover it in your weekly one-on-one.
- You may want to give them time to collect their thoughts. If it's important enough to ask them, it is important enough to get the right answer (just the facts).
- Know when to leave well enough alone. Sometimes we overexplain, overapologize, or overanalyze. Let people have enough time to think about what has been said.
- Recognize and refocus team members to defuse employee conflicts. If you are aware of a conflict among your team members, take steps to separate, bring together, or otherwise improve the employees' relationships.
- Do not let others take advantage of—or make unrealistic demands of—your team or other team members.
- Always take pride in your team.
- Know your own communication style. Work to improve areas that are not as strong as others.
- Control your body language—it can turn people off.
- Forward your calls to voice mail when unavailable.
- Lock the keyboard on your PC and do not read e-mails or instant messages while meeting with someone.

- Think about what you are saying before you open your mouth (you cannot take words back once they are spoken).
- Do not get frustrated if someone does not understand what you are telling him or her. Try a different way or explain to a third party and let that person present it in a different light.
- When someone is venting, do not interrupt or become defensive.
- Do not bring a laptop to a meeting unless you are using it to present information—you need to focus on the meeting.

Helpful hints: You can use these small techniques to improve communications and foster respect.

Total Quality Management

Total Quality Management (TQM), International Standards Organization (ISO 9000) and Information Technology Infrastructure Library (ITIL) certifications were very big initiatives in the 1980s—and possibly are a big part of how you operate today. Simply put, if you document the process and follow the process every time, you will get consistent results. The quality of the product or service is dependent on how well your process is defined. You can document a bad process, get consistent results, and not deliver a quality product or service. This has been statistically proven over the years—and is still true today.

Definitions:

- Suppliers—anyone who provides input into a specific process.
- Process—the action taken to achieve the desired results.
- Customer—the person or team that receives the output of the process.

These simple steps can get you on the road to a quality delivery system:

- Document the process from your view.
- Build the process with your customers and suppliers to get buy-in.

- Agree on the new process or the modifications to the existing process.
- Document and communicate the process to anyone that will use the process.
- Implement a change-control process for all future processes, changes, modifications, or retirement so that everyone knows what to do.

When you document a process, you need to make sure that every person or team that uses that process is a part of the documentation process. Most teams that do not follow these simple guidelines end up spending an enormous amount of time trying to convince someone to use the process. When they are a part of the documentation process, they accept it. It should not be looked at as extra work, but rather how I do my job. When you change the culture of your company and embrace quality, everyone wins. Those of us who have been in IT for twenty or thirty years have seen many things come and go over the years. I have noticed that trends in the industry repeat themselves every ten years or so. We have seen things such as layoffs called downsizing or rightsizing. Someone will come up with a new buzzword from time to time, but many times the event is the same—it is just called something different. We have seen trends in outsourcing over the years. When management is not happy with either performance or profit, they can move it from within the company to an outsource company. If they do not get the results they want after moving it, many companies have been known to bring it back in-house. We have seen off-shoring to foreign countries in an attempt to save money or to free up full-time resources. We have seen data centers decentralized to put the data closer the customers, and we have seen decentralized computing consolidated back into huge data centers. We have seen the large data center mainframes give way to the client-server world. There will always be emotional discussions around one large mainframe versus multiple client servers. Some continue in the client-server world, and some bring back the mainframe data centers. We have seen the dumb terminal replaced by the PC in an attempt to improve the customer experience. Over the years, we have seen TQM tools in support of excellence like ISO, Six Sigma, and ITIL.

The bottom line is that many of the basic tools from twenty or thirty years ago are the same—they are just called something different. Unless we embrace the concepts, we are doomed to be mediocre. Things such as system availability and stability for our end customers continue to be goals of our companies as they have been for the past thirty years. No matter what you call it—and no matter how you document or define it—repeatable processes are the key to our success. Leaders find ways to make sure that their teams can execute their jobs flawlessly.

Total quality management: Set the tone to help change how your company looks at and handles defects.

Root-Cause Analysis

We talked earlier about the glass being half full or half empty. When processes are designed, tested, monitored, modified, and repeated, the results should be the desired outcome. We all know that machines can fail, and people can make mistakes. Things change every day and it is possible that processes that were implemented a few months or years earlier can fail because the environment has changed. We always have to monitor our results to ensure that we are still getting our desired outcome. What we should always strive for is 100 percent compliance. Most people will say we had 99.9 percent system availability—isn't that awesome? And, the answer is yes. That is good, but what about the .1 percent? If you are able to keep the system stable at 99.9 percent, just imagine the added capability you can give to your customers if you can eliminate the other .1 percent. Downtime to your customers—no matter how small—is negatively affecting the company's bottom line. I worked for a company that had multiple call centers for external customer support. Any time the online system was down, the representatives would have to tell the customer to call back later, or they would have to write down the customer's information. Once the systems came back up, all that data would have to be entered into the system by offline representatives. This could cause a huge overtime impact for the company, depending on the length of the outage. Just imagine the work involved if your company had thirty or forty million customers. This would be a negative experience for the external customers who could impact their decision to keep your company as a provider. It is a known fact that if you do not fix the root causes of a problem, it will recur. I had an instructor in a quality class one time that really put it in perspective for me. Everyone was saying how 99.9 percent was a really good system availability percentage. He posed a simple question: How would you feel about an airline that strived for 99.9 percent successful landings and you were on the .1 percent flight?

Leaders know that anything less than 100 percent means that their teams and they have work to do. A good example is a car using too much oil. You can make it work by refilling the oil when it is low. This is not very costly—and is an option that many people choose. They have to watch the oil level closely every time they use the vehicle to make sure that they do not burn up the motor. Remember that this does not address the problem—it is only addressing the symptom. (This would be the 99.9 percent.) What we need to do is get a qualified mechanic to find the root cause of the problem. It can be anything from a loose oil cap, an oil filter that needs tightening, or the motor could need a major overhaul. (This would be the .1 percent.) If we are able to fix the real problem with the oil leak, then we can focus our attention on other things and only check it every two thousand miles. Until you investigate the root cause, it is going to be a problem that will require someone's attention. Processes that are not working correctly or break down can be costly to your company as well. Wouldn't it be better for that person to spend his or her energy on a new project?

Many tools of quality can be used specifically for this purpose. You may elect to train your team or bring in a quality specialist to drive the project. Either way, quality is something that every member of your team should have at the top of his or her To Do List. (See the Continuous Improvement chapter, where people are encouraged to think outside of the box.)

Root–cause analysis: Look past the problem's symptoms—search out and correct the underlying causes.

Continuous Improvement

If you do not have time to do it right the first time, how will you find the time to do it over? In today's world, two major factors challenge us. Either there are not enough resources to do the job or the cost of getting it done surpasses the estimate. This is why it is so important that resources are working on the right things. If they are working on the right things—and they are doing it right—then the outcome is going to be good.

Doing a poor job or doing the wrong things will have a huge impact on the bottom line. Someone is going to have to clean up the mess, and the cost of a second resource added to the project will only drive you further away from the goal of on time and on budget. Being able to measure your success will help you determine whether process improvements are warranted.

Once you understand the concept, it is not something extra—it is how you do your job. We should always strive to stamp out defects and rework. Quality starts with you and filters to your team. By being a role model for quality, you set clear expectations that being average is not enough. We should always work with the philosophy that the customer comes first. If we build quality into our daily activities, we will be able to consistently deliver a quality product. Being able to understand the requirements is critical to planning and building processes that prevent defects. Quality happens through people—and it is your responsibility to coach and train your team members. Quality improvements never end and should be part of your daily activity to ensure that your team, your company, and you are the best each can be. One of the best tools I have found is brainstorming. Brainstorming is a group technique designed to generate large numbers of ideas for the solution or a problem. It can be used to solve problems or come up with new ideas. Even though one person can use it, the results are much better when it is used by a group of three to ten folks. The more diversified the group, the better. You have more points of view represented due to their previous experiences. We know what we know—and we do not know what we do not know.

When I am looking to solve a problem or build a new process, I like to involve people who deal with the day-to-day issues. Who better to find out how things really work than from the people in the trenches. I always hated it when I would get a new policy or procedure from corporate that did not take into account the remote offices. Your process is only as good as the people you have building it through the brainstorming process. If you try to do it yourself, you only hinder the progress of the process by limiting the breadth of the solution by your limited knowledge of the subject matter.

You want to start by gathering a diverse group of people in a room with a whiteboard and/or flip charts. (Brainstorming is possible remotely, but you must have an experienced brainstorming team and tools that allow visibility to the material being gathered.)

- Explain what you are attempting to accomplish (find root cause, build new process, etc.).
- Capture all comments on the board or flip charts.
- Stress to the team that there are no bad ideas and encourage all ideas.
- No one makes fun of anyone or anything brought up.
- Nothing is eliminated during the brainstorming sessions.
- When all ideas have been logged, then discussions begin on each one to determine feasibility of each issue relevant to the goal.
- You work through each item on the list and eliminate any that do not support the goal. When this is completed, you will have a list of items that will support achieving your goal.

- You will need to prioritize the items on the list so that your efforts are focused on the right actions.

Note: When building your priority list of items, you need to determine how you want to accomplish your goals:

- Quickest
- Easiest
- Least cost to implement
- Biggest benefit to the business
- Low-hanging fruit

You may have other criteria—specific to your company—but you get the picture. Once you have your priority list completed, you will have an action plan ready to go. It is best to understand what resources you have available to work the project before you start. Most companies may only have enough resources to work on one task at a time. If this is the case, start with number one on the task list and work your way down. Be sure to give updates after each task is completed. If you are fortunate enough to have additional resources available, you may be able to work more than one task at a time. Be sure not to start too many tasks at the same time. It is important that you consider whether tasks can be completed without affecting other tasks. It may be better to start and finish each task and communicate your success before moving to the next task. Showing progress is important to management, but make sure that you do not start too many tasks and not complete any of them—that is a pitfall you want to avoid. When you show progress, you open up the possibility of receiving additional funding and support, when needed.

Regardless of the problem you are brainstorming, remember these basic quality steps as you seek to implement a solution:

Quality is Customer Driven

- Understand your customers' business.
- Determine what their requirements are.

- Work with them as partners.

Definition of a Process

- Define inputs (both your customers' and your requirements).
- Create your goal to exceed their expectations or tickle your customers.
- Define process.
- Define outputs (both for your customers and for requirements).

Flowcharts

- A flowchart is a pictorial representation showing all of the steps of a process.
- A flowchart should be written at a level that allows someone unfamiliar with the process to understand it.

Process Analysis

- Clarify
- Simplify
- Reduce cycle time
- Automate the process

Root-Cause Analysis Measurement Tools

- Tracking the problem
- Pareto
- Histogram
- Scatter Diagrams
- Control Charts

You want to fix the cause, not the symptoms. Problems or failures that are not fixed properly will return repeatedly. This leads to lost productivity and can be very expensive to your company.

Continuous improvement of processes is a never-ending cycle. It can be challenging for many companies. You are going to change the culture of the company on how it looks at defects. You will need the commitment of your management team and your team members. It will not happen overnight, but it will pay tremendous benefits to the company.

Continuous improvement: Take the lead in identifying process, root cause, and customer-driving factors for an ailing project.

Problem Solving

There are natural problem solvers and then there are those who may need to add that skill to their toolbox. Most team members and teams are successful when they brainstorm the problem-solving process together. Attempting to solve problems in a vacuum limits the actual number of available solutions. Each of our experiences gives us important input into problem solving. The more diverse the team, the more potential solutions will be explored. Managers have a high-level view of issues that may be fine in some cases. I truly believe that the team members who perform the task have the best details of the actual process. The workers may have the best ideas about how to solve the issues. They deal with it day in and day out. They also will accept the changes with less resistance if they are a part of the solution. You can compare it with someone being force-fed or willing to eat on his or her own. Someone that has helped to prepare the meal is more likely to eat it and not turn up their nose at it. Imagine the productivity improvements when both those performing the tasks and those involved in building the solution accept changes. Sounds like a win-win to me. Asking someone's opinions and agreeing are two different things. Listening to someone else's opinion can force us all to think (sometimes outside of our comfort zone). Keep in mind that asking for opinions does not mean that you agree with them. It may be that the solution is a result of several opinions—that is something that you cannot get when you solve problems by yourself. Many managers may think that asking for someone's opinion is a sign of weakness or could make them look silly. Your role as a manager is to interpret opinions and to respond with the best solution to the problem. When it comes down to it, is it more important to be the one whose solution is used, or is it better being a part of the team that arrives at the best solution? It takes a mature manager to be professional enough to be unafraid to do what is right for the team or company—even if it means not using his or her own idea. Show your appreciation for input from others.

I once had an insecure manager that would be aware of an issue and immediately put together a solution and implement it. He felt, because he had done the job several years earlier, that he knew how to solve the problems. What he did not realize was that the job had changed significantly since he had been in the position. He struggled with his ego—that his people may know better than he did about the current environment and what it would take to fix the issue. He also liked to keep everything secret and seldom would share information or ask for input. He would create a new process and roll it out as a new policy without ever talking to his customers or peers that had to use the new process. His behavior was counterproductive and created conflicts and hard feelings within the department. Note: Remember to get people involved when you are building a new process or policy. If they provide input to the process, perform the process, or get output from the process, they should have representation in the brainstorming process. As previously mentioned, people will use processes that they helped build and resist those that are shoved down their throats.

Many of the changes he made were ineffective because he did not know or care that his customers or peers should have been involved. This created many costly reworks and delays in getting a good process to the teams. Do not let this happen to you.

Problem solving: Involve all the team members—even if they have dissenting or differing opinions.

Dealing with Stress

How do you deal with stress? Divorce and alcoholism have become two very common results of stressful jobs. As with any disorder, stress will creep up on you without warning. It can be in the form of gaining weight, not sleeping well, high blood pressure, or any number of other forms. Knowing that you have it is not always easy. It is easier to see how stress is impacting someone else than ourselves. We all need release valves for stress. Some may jog, spend hours in the gym, walk, read, or spend time with their kids. How you deal with stress is not as important as making sure that you deal with it. Stress is a killer. If you do not have a release valve, find one. Your future will depend on it.

Tip: Stopping by the bar and drinking every night is not necessarily a proven way to relieve stress.

I once worked with a person who would spend two to three hours a night drinking in a bar before going home to his family. This was his way of dealing with stress of the job, a wife, and two kids who were out of control. This continued for years and ended up causing him serious medical problems. Finding a stress release valve is critical, but make sure it is not more dangerous than stress itself.

Letting stress flow off your back like water off a duck's back may seem easier said than done. The following information helps me: Letting go does not mean that you do not care. It just means that you have done everything humanly possible to make it work. On your way home, tell yourself, "I did my best today." When you walk in that door at home, leave the stress outside. Stress is the emotional and physical wear and tear of responding to the pressures, changes, and demands of life. Stress can play a major role in families. I also feel that it is very important to get an annual physical. As we mature (my way of saying as we get older), it is important that we detect and monitor our bodies more closely. We were all indestructible when we were young, but we need to find and address any health issues as soon as possible as we mature. Early detection can truly be a life-saving event.

Balance in your life. Every generation says it, and I believe it is true in every case. Each generation faces more and more distractions and stressors. I have worked in the corporate world for close to forty years, and I have seen more than my share of examples. I have seen executives who traveled so much that it destroyed their marriage and their kids. They were seldom home, and the spouse could not handle the kids or just got tired of trying. I have seen the climb up the corporate ladder claim more than one marriage. The spouse was so blinded by promotions that eighty-hour weeks became the norm. They were expected to work weekends on a regular basis, and many times they missed dance recitals, track meets, or ball games. By the time some woke up, their kids were grown and out of the house. In some cases, they never did realize what they had missed. You see single parents working hard to keep the family together, and they are to be commended. Between the demands of the job, the family, and yourself, there is often not enough time in the day. My philosophy is that you have to have balance in your life. Just as you recharge your cell phone or PC, you have to recharge your personal battery and relationships with your loved ones.

I worked for a company where my team was so loyal to the company—and to me—that they would never take vacation time. When I researched our vacation bank time, I found that 60 percent of my team had more than three hundred hours of vacation time on the books. I called my entire management team together and said *we* have a problem. I explained my concerns of burning the team out. I gave them a goal to reduce each team member's vacation time by 20 percent by the end of the year. Then I set a goal for the next year not to have anyone with more than 160 hours on the books. It was not easy, but the management team responded and made it a priority in their weekly meeting with their teams. In the monthly All-Hands meeting, I would ask who had taken an interesting vacation or had one planned and let them share it with their peers. Once the team realized that we were serious about them taking time off and that it was okay, they started to buy into it. The team became more relaxed, refreshed, and performed better because they were less stressed.

You are only human—and sometimes you just cannot do everything. I had a manager that I supported who cared deeply for his team. We worked through some hard times together—everything from terminating good people who got themselves into a bad situation to relocating the team out of state. In some cases, I may not have agreed with decisions being handed down, but as a part of management, I had to support it. Once I had come to grips that I had done everything I could to help the team, I was able accept the challenge and move on. I was still very respectful of the people involved, but I had to detach myself from the emotion of the event. My manager had a hard time understanding how I could manage to do that. I explained that being a people person is both a blessing and a curse.

It is a blessing because it lets you get to know people at a different level than most executives want. At the same time, it can be a curse. When you become closer to someone and you have to deliver bad news, it is difficult. It is important to understand that managing it does not mean stopping caring about people. When I look in the mirror before I go to bed, I have to know that I have done everything within my power to treat everyone involved with dignity and respect. Until you can do that, stress will rule your life.

We all have different ways to release stress. I once worked with a guy who would spend his family vacation at the beach. His wife would sunbathe, and he would sit under an umbrella and read technical books. He would read ten or twelve different books each vacation. I do not know if you have ever read a technical manual, but for most folks, it would be lights out (bedtime reading). I once jokingly told him that he was a sick individual. How in the world could you relax reading those types of books after spending sixty hours a week in a stressful job? He explained that the technical books took him away from his normal daily stressors. He would forget everything going on at the office and update his technical skills at the same time. He said that his wife enjoyed her time, which made him happy, and he would always come back to work relaxed and ready to jump back into the fire. This is a great example of the multiple ways for people to relieve stress. Whether it is reading, attending plays, golfing, jogging, or playing chess, it does not really matter—just find one that works for you.

Dealing with stress: Rate your own stress factors and your ability to release and let go.

Symptoms of Stress

- Unusual voice volume—vocal explosiveness
- Nervous tics or habits (tapping etc.)
- Vibration feeling (like a motor running)
- Laryngitis
- Frequent headaches
- Migraine headaches and symptoms
- Numbness in extremities
- Repeated lateness
- Repeated forgetfulness
- Rapid heartbeat
- Rigid thinking, dogmatism
- Sudden weight change
- Insomnia
- Use of combative gestures
- Use of sarcasm
- Use of exaggeration in speech
- Hostile language
- Breathing problems (shortness of breath)
- Misperception (failing to hear or see accurately)
- Blowing up/loss of temper
- Losing perspective (mountain versus molehill)
- Unusual amount of blinking or yawning
- Excessive illness/frequency of colds
- Sudden change in diet (binging)
- Eating too fast

Anybody may have some of these symptoms at any given moment. A combination of several of these symptoms may begin to suggest overstress. Look for patterns of symptoms and seek a competent physician or mental health practitioner.

Years ago, I read an article on stress that said we really have three options when it comes to dealing with stress. We can alter it by addressing or solving the issue. We can try to avoid it by letting go or just saying no. If neither of these options works for you, the last option is to accept it by building our resistance and changing our perception. If all else fails, you may need to move on to another job or different personal situation.

Sixty-Second Tension Tamers

- Yawn and sigh
- Stretch
- Sedentary stretch
- Triple shake
- Deep muscle relaxation: make a fist with both hands, relax—repeat ten times
- Make fists and raise them over your shoulders, bring hands back down to side relaxing fists—repeat ten times
- Raise shoulders (tense neck)—repeat ten times
- Raise your eyebrows, relax—repeat ten times
- Squeeze eyes closed, open—repeat ten times
- Press your lips together then release—repeat ten times
- Take a deep breath, hold it for five seconds, exhale—repeat ten times
- Tense stomach muscles, relax—repeat ten times
- Point your feet away from you, stretch your legs, relax—repeat ten times

Symptoms of stress: Be aware of the signs—for you and those around you.

Support Your Team

Coaching requires practice and an open mind. You owe it to your team to coach them on how to keep cool while dealing with disgruntled customers. They also need to know how to deal with the pressures of stress and being pulled in multiple directions at once. When your team stays professional, you can support them. I once had a computer operator who ran a report and delivered it to one of his customers. The customer was not happy because the report did not give them the information they were looking for. The customer started chewing out the operator, and they got into a huge fight. Both sides spoke some harsh words, and we all ended up in the VP's office. In the end, both the customer and the operator were put on performance plans because of their unprofessional behavior. If my operator had kept his cool and had turned the issue over to me to resolve, I could have supported him. When the operator lost control and overreacted, my hands were tied. Even if the operator made a mistake, I could have backed him—but when he lost his composure with the customer, it was out of my hands. He should have told the customer that he was sorry that the report was wrong and he would bring the issue to me. This would have taken him out of the middle and given me a chance to investigate the issue. He fell into the age old trap of taking it personally and getting emotionally involved with the customer.

Never be afraid to hire team members that are smarter than you are. When hiring, always keep in perspective the good of the team, the department, and the company. Hiring someone with great technical skills, but that lacks the needed chemistry to mesh with the team or company, will not benefit anyone. I like to use the team-interview process for prospective new hires. Even though you have the final approval, the team can give you a good indication of how the candidate will fit in. They also feel good about you valuing their opinions. A leader will hire to the team's weakness. You can never be afraid to hire someone that has had different experiences. A good team will have different tool sets and experiences that can really add to the team's ability to handle a larger variety of issues. The more the diverse the team, the stronger the team can be in solving issues and putting together big-picture solutions.

At least every six months, schedule time with team members to talk about their career growth. This can sometimes be difficult because you will need to talk about areas that need to be improved. Always be sincere and honest in this type of discussion. Understanding their goals and their current tool set will help you determine what skills will need to be upgraded for that next promotion or opportunity. Many times, we focus on the technical skills sets and forget about the people skills. Have you ever known any technical people who could not talk to customers without confusing them or talking down to them? It may not be their fault; they need to be given the opportunity to grow. When you give them the tools for their toolbox to grow, you both benefit. Every team member should own the responsibility for their career growth. However, as managers, we should be a part of the solution by doing everything we can to get them the tools that they need.

Here is a difficult opportunity. What do you do if they do not have a career path within your department? Keep working them until they quit? No. Instead, consider helping them find another position somewhere else within the company. The logic behind this approach is simple. If they have been a reliable team contributor for a significant period of time, why not give another department a good resource. If they stay within the company, the company wins. If they leave the company—and eventually they will—the company will lose a good worker. This is hard because replacing that person may cause some discomfort for your team. They have been there, doing a good job, and the role they played has been solid. However, if you look at it as an opportunity to add something new to their toolbox, the other department gets a proven performer and you get to bring in fresh talent—doesn't everyone win? We have to step back and look at the big picture; sometimes that can mean some big challenges. It is about doing the right thing for the team member, the team, and the company. It shows your maturity as a leader.

You may never know when an opportunity for advancement will occur. When it does, the person who is most ready for it will probably get it. When a job opens up is not the time to start thinking about adding the skill to your toolbox. You have to have a goal or plan for where you want to go next in your career. Once you know what that is, start working on getting the training you need to be ready. This can be formal training paid for by the company or yourself, depending on your company's training budget. Another inexpensive tool I like to use is called the shadow program. In the Shadow Program, the manager works out a deal with a peer manager to let team members spend time with one of the other manager's team members. I would let my help desk, computer operator, or desktop support folks spend four hours a week with NT administrators, database administrators (DBAs), or network specialists. They would find out all about a job—and help them decide if it would be an interesting career for them. Over the years, this approach has helped more than a hundred team members get to the next level. It shows that there is an interest by the team member; it also builds a strong relationship with the specialist who will know quickly if the person has the ability to learn the skill for the new position. When an opening occurs, the specialist knows the candidate better—and the specialist can put in a good word to the hiring manager. It is our job as leaders to help our team members be ready for the next step. The ultimate responsibility belongs to the individual team members, but a good leader can guide and assist them in their quest.

Another way to support your team is to stay in tune with what they are working on and in tune with the progress that is being made. If you do not already receive a weekly status report, maybe you should require one. It can be as simple as:

- Accomplishments during the past week (things completed)
- Planned activities for next week
- Issues (things that they need your assistance on)

This simple status report can be modified to fit your particular environment. They should be concise. One thing I have learned is that the farther up the ladder you are, the less time you have for details. A little or a lot of effort can be put into status reporting. It may be better to do high-level status reports. That way, the manager can ask for details on specific projects if additional information is needed. This approach saves work for both the team member and the manager.

I have had great success having weekly staff meeting with my direct reports. By getting together for one hour a week, I can communicate team information. At the end, give each of them five minutes to share what is going on with their individual teams or issues that they are dealing with that may affect their peers. It is amazing how beneficial it can be to the entire team. This allows everyone on your team to stay on the same page in relationship to the team and the company priorities.

In addition to the weekly staff meetings, I do weekly one-on-one meetings. These are regularly scheduled thirty-minute meetings with my direct reports. We can discuss confidential information or issues about the team, their customers, or their individual performance. This is where you give coaching if necessary and give them a chance to discuss specifics on issues or projects.

In one case, I supported more than two hundred people nationwide, but I was lucky if I had face-to-face time with them each year. To compensate for this, I would have monthly all-hands conference calls with the entire team. We would discuss upcoming projects as well as the current direction of the company and our teams. We would recognize our top performers for the month, and then we would open up the meeting to questions and answers. Anyone on the team could ask questions of the managers or me. If we did not have the answer, we would take a note and respond to the team with the answer once it was researched. This was my way of giving my remote team members an extension of my open-door policy. Your ability to conduct these types of meetings will depend on your specific situation. If you have ten or more direct reports, you may have to spread the weekly one-on-one sessions to every other week. My point is that regularly scheduled meetings with your direct reports and their teams can pay tremendous benefits. It truly shows that you are committed to them and to the success of their teams.

True leaders will make the time!

Support your team: Check the team progress and encourage team members in career advancements.

Get to Know

It is important to know your team, their family members (or pets), their interests, and their challenges. Remember the last time your boss asked you how your significant other, child, or pet was doing. How did that make you feel? Without crossing over the line and intruding, you can still learn about your team members' families and interests.Knowing your individual team members and their performance history can be a big help during difficult times. For example, you have a very dependable team member who recently has been coming in consistently late. When you talk to him, does he seem to be either in a daze or focused on something else. If you do not take the time to know your team members, you could just assume that this performance issue is just that. But in reality, when you talk to him, you find out that he just had a baby and is taking on the night feedings. How you deal with these types of issues will help mold the type of person you are. When you have a solid performer, but the performance becomes erratic, there is usually a good reason. It is in the best interest of the team member, yourself, and the company to work through the issue. There is only a fifty-fifty chance when you hire someone from the outside that they are as good as their résumé says they are. You owe it to yourself and your team to support your reliable team members through the peaks and valleys of performance. (See Corrective Action chapter for helpful hints.)

Getting to know your customers, peers, and teams is one of the best ways to build strong relationships. The more you know about them and their challenges, the better equipped you are to provide better solutions to their issues. I worked for a company that had retail stores nationwide. Every year, the directors and VPs would spend a week in the retail stores to gain a better understanding of the retail teams' challenges. They would see, firsthand, issues on a daily basis. They would give daily updates on a conference call, and all issues were logged. When completed, the issues lists were reviewed by executives from the retail and IT groups to determine what fix or changes could improve the experience for our customers in the stores. This was a very successful program—and it really made you appreciate your remote team members. As I have mentioned before, being remote is a much different world than working in the head office. By spending time with our retail team members, we were able to understand how we can help our customers.

One of the easiest ways to get to know your customers is to schedule visits so that you can get to know them. How can you provide world class service to your customers if you do not know their environment and challenges? You need to spend time with them to understand their business. I like to use the shadow program, where you spend a day or two a month with your customer. It gives you a chance to see their operations, ask questions about why they do what they do, and discuss how you can assist them in achieving their performance goals. Meeting with them on a weekly, monthly, or quarterly basis can only help improve relationships between your organizations. These sessions can be to meet with the management team and hold meetings with subsets of their teams. During such meetings, I would give a short presentation on my team and what we do. Then I would turn the meeting over to my customers and ask each one around the table to tell me one thing my team does well and something that they would like us to improve upon. When you have an open and honest relationship with your customers, you will be amazed by how much valuable information you can obtain. This information, when taken back to your team, will help you determine how you can provide better service to your customers. Many years ago, I was a part of an IT group that redesigned and wrote a new order-entry system. We spent almost two years getting it ready for production. When we did the final review with the customer, they said that they did not want it. It did not address their needs. Looking into the issues, we found that the IT analyst had built the perfect order-entry system, but had failed to work with the customers on what the customers needed. From that day forward, I have always remembered to include the customer and what they need before starting down the action plan path.

Get to know: While respecting boundaries, learn about your team members and peers.

Open-Door Policy

Many managers say they have an open-door policy, but do they really? An open-door policy only works when the manager is mature and professional enough to live it. When you have built trust with your team members, they will feel comfortable talking to you. You need to let them come in, close the door, and vent if they need to. Sometimes, *you* may be the cause of their frustrations. You have to be mature enough to let them talk without fear of repercussions. By providing them with an honest discourse with boundaries, you show them that you are sincere about their concerns. You have to be sincere when explaining difficult subjects. You have to listen and be respectful of the speaker. You need to stay in control and not become defensive. They will talk with their peers about their experience. If you are walking the walk and talking the talk, it will show and you will truly have an open-door policy. When your teams know that you accept being human, and are capable of mistakes, they will feel more at ease. Being able to listen to constructive criticism—and turn it into something positive for the team—makes a great statement for both you and your team.I have seen managers who say they have an open-door policy—as long as you did not bring up anything that reflected poorly on them. I had a boss once that went off the deep end and proceeded to tell me how an issue was entirely my fault. As they used to say, he handed me my head on a platter. Needless to say, I never darkened his door again. I have also had a leader who was a 180 degree difference from this guy. He listened to my concerns, asked clarifying questions, and asked how I thought he should have handled it. He then explained why he had done what he did and why. This approach completely blew me away. I knew that he cared what people really thought and was trying to do the right thing. When we finished, he thanked me for bringing the issue to him and asked me to come back if I had any other issues. He did not take it personally and did not try to turn it back on me. It takes a mature leader to truly have an open-door policy. If you ask for feedback, you have to be able to take the good and the not-so-good remarks. Be careful what you ask for—you may get it.

Feedback is a gift. Use it constructively to make things better.

Open-door policy: Allow for confidential venting that may be directed at you by upset coworkers.

Goal Setting

Ever think of setting goals in your personal life? How about a goal of losing twenty pounds or reading more to improve yourself? Instead of spending five hours a night in front of the television, maybe start that hobby you have been thinking about for years. How about spending one hour per night of quality time with family? We all get comfortable and do not want to step outside of our comfort zone. Remember that you add skills to your toolbox when you do something new.

Goals can help you achieve your personal, professional, short-term, and long-term objectives. Goals can be as simple or as complex as you like. Make the goals fit your needs or lifestyle. Achieving those goals on a consistent basis can go a long way toward getting you happiness, success, and/or advancements.

You are probably used to seeing goal-setting with company goals, but do not forget that career and personal goals are equally important. We can be so wrapped up in our jobs that we lose track of everything else. Being able to have a balance between the goals will make you a better person and performer. Without goals, you will never know if you have accomplished what you set out for.

Early in my career, I was very focused on the job. I was not as focused on my family as I should have been. The IT profession can be very a demanding career; if you let it, it will consume you. I was so wrapped up with my job that I truly lost ten years of my life because I was not properly focused on my family. Significant emotional events will trigger changes in people. It can be a death in a family, a divorce, bankruptcy, or any number of different events.

It was such an event that led to my aha moment. I lost my older brother when I was in my twenties and realized that I had missed many opportunities to tell him I loved him. From that day forward, I have never said good-bye to family or friends without letting them know I care about them. I changed jobs so that I would not have to travel as much and could be home more with my wife and kids. I made it a point to get to as many basketball games and track meets as possible. I never missed a dance recital or birthday party from that time forward. Family and friends became the most important thing in the world to me. I realized that life is too short not to be happy—and I made a personal goal that my family would come first for the rest of my life.

I had someone come talk to me because he was miserable in his job. He had been there ten years and hated to go to work each day. He had worked his way up into management, but he still had not found happiness. He saw things that could be improved, but the owner wanted nothing to do with it. He wanted to improve things we take for granted—conducting annual reviews, documenting processes for dealing with human resources (HR) issues, and giving raises. I coached him on ways to present things to the owner; maybe he would get different results. He tried that for a couple of months, but had no success. We spoke again and I explained that everyone has a different level of pain tolerance. When the pain becomes intolerable, people will make those hard decisions. I suggested that he pick a date three to six months in the future and put a stake in the ground. If things were not better by then, he would need to make one of two decisions: he was going to have to be willing to live with it for the rest of his life or he was going to have to leave the company. He took my advice, and, six months later, he turned in his resignation. He started his own company and said that he was never going to make the same mistakes as his old boss. He is a much happier person today—and he is able to enjoy his family more than he ever would have working for his old boss.

Balance between family and work is critical to everyone's well-being. You need to have personal and career goals for where you want to be in two to five years. Only you can choose what that balance is. Are you up to the challenge?

Goal Setting: Set a short-term or long-term goal whether personal or professional.

Hiring Practices

One of any manager's biggest challenges is hiring good people. Some do it by the seat of their pants; others have methods to their madness. It is important to have a good job description. Explaining what work, education, and skill sets are required will make the hiring process much smoother. You would not hire a good technical person for a job requiring extremely high people skills or vice versa. You want to make sure that the candidate can fit into the chemistry of the current team. Because of changes in the law, you cannot ask many things during interviews (check with your human resources department for restrictions). During my career, I have had the opportunity to manage a systems programming group in a mainframe environment. We were running CICS (online application for Customer Care Team) at our company. We had been seeing some slowdown in the response time for a few days. Our customers were reporting the issue to our help desk, and we had assigned the ticket to our top CICS programmer to investigate. You need to understand that this person was one of the five most brilliant IT folks I have worked with in almost forty years. When he was not monitoring the systems, he was reading technical manuals on the system. When he was not reading manuals, he was on the system monitoring it. When he left work for the day, he would go home and log on to monitor the system (no life balance, but that is another story for another time). Anyway, you get the picture; he was very good technically and dedicated as the day is long. I had only been managing him a few weeks and did not have a lot of familiarity with his customer-interfacing skills. I asked him to go over to one of the customer service representatives to see the issue firsthand. He had already spent a few hours researching the issue, but he really did not have any leads as to the root cause. A short time later, I received a call from the customer service representative's manager saying there was a problem. She told me how my CICS programmer had her representative in tears. When the programmer returned, I called him into my office, closed the door, and asked him to tell me what he found out. He said nothing really; he watched the representative do some transactions, asked her some questions, and then left. I thanked him and went to meet with the customer service representative and her manager. She said that he was talking down to her, asking her what she was doing wrong and why she was doing it this way and not that way. He had asked her how long she had been a representative and whether she had gone through training. If you have ever seen the computer guy on Saturday Night Live skits, you get the picture. The end user was having computer problems and placed a call to the help desk. The computer guy shows up, pushes the customer out of the way, keys in a bunch of commands and the problem is resolved. The computer guys says, "Any two year old should have know that." Then the computer guys leaves and the customer is sitting there asking what the heck just happened? I learned a big lesson that day. The programmer spent ten to twelve hours per day reading manuals and monitoring systems with little to no interface with people. He really did not mean to make her feel badly, but he was data-driven and peeled out anything that was not black and white. He would ask a question and expect a concise answer without background or emotion. After that experience, I was very selective about sending a techie to speak with the customer without being there as well. I would accompany them to the customer; if I saw the conversation going sideways, I would step in and redirect the conversation. After the meeting, I would take the programmer back to my office, close the door, and explain why I had done what I did. I also set up mandatory soft skills training for all of my techies. Slowly but surely, they got better meeting with their customers. It is kind of like public speaking—if you do not practice it, you are never going to get good at it. Leaders have to pay attention to the details and help coach their people.

Make sure to hire for the right skill set when looking to add valuable resources to your team. For positions with high stress levels or long hours, it is important to ask how they relieve stress. Disaster is just down the road if people do not have a release valve for stress. You want to make it clear about travel if the position calls for it. There is nothing worse than hiring someone that you need to travel only to find out that they cannot or will not travel. I truly feel that peer interviews pay big dividends. Most teams will not be threatened by the candidate, but they will pick up on things that the manager might not. The other avenue that I strongly recommend is to look internally within the company. If you have a strong candidate that has a proven track record with the company, it is a big plus for hiring. They will know the culture of the company—and the time needed to bring them up to speed on the job can be significantly reduced. Try to promote from within your company. When you hire someone off the street, you have a fifty-fifty chance that the candidate is as good as his or her résumé says he or she is.

Hiring practices: Consider hiring from within and do not be afraid to hire people smarter than you.

Reviews, Promotions, and Merit Increases

Have you ever worked at a company where you did not get a review on time—or even worse, you did not get one at all? How did that make you feel? Review time is the time of the year that every manager has to do whatever it takes to make sure that his or her team members are taken care of properly. Most companies spend the entire year working on major projects—both scheduled and unscheduled. We ask our people to be motivated, supportive, and energetic. They work long hours, including nights and weekends, to make sure that our projects are completed on time. How much trust or respect can team members have for their manager or the company if they cannot get their reviews on time? As managers, we must take ownership of the process and ensure that reviews are completed on time.

During my career, I have always stayed at companies between five and thirteen years. I have seen so many managers that do not make reviews and notification of pay increases a priority that I have lost count. However, in one case, I worked for a vice president who told me what he wanted from my team and let me do my job. He would send me my review and paperwork to ensure meeting the deadlines (we were remote from each other). He would find time to discuss any questions that I had about it. I have also worked for VPs that never found the time to conduct reviews with me or send me the paperwork. I would find out about my increase by the direct deposit made to my checking account. I believe that this is very disrespectful to the employee. Most directors and VPs did not start out that way. I believe that they were very good at what they did early in their careers and rose through the ranks to get to their level. There was always a joke about people having to lose brain cells to become a director or VP. I am here to tell you that true leaders will never forget the little things they did well when they were middle managers. Leaders set examples. If you are a director or VP, you are going to expect your managers to meet the review deadlines the right way. Do not accept anything less from yourself.

Tips for a successful review process:

- Thirty to sixty days before the review is due, ask the team member for a list of his or her past year's accomplishments and a list of his or her top ten customers.
- Send e-mails to the customers, requesting feedback on the team member's performance.
- Ask the team member to do a self-assessment.
- Fifteen to thirty days before the review is due, write your draft of the review and set it aside. Keep in mind that you want to identify both positive and negative performance.
- Ten to fifteen days before the review is due, reread the review and make any final changes to the draft. Make three copies: one for the team member, one for HR, and one for your file.
- Seven days before the review is due, schedule a thirty-minute review meeting with the team member.
- The day of the review, give the team member a copy of the review and walk them through the details. Explaining the ratings and the comments will help them understand why they are being rated the way they are. Field questions that the team member may have so that there is a complete understanding of the review.

Note: I will not penalize anyone for anything that I have not had a coaching session with him or her on during the past year. If I did not do my job by telling people, I will not hold them responsible for that aspect of their performance. Do you remember a review that you received or gave where there was strong disagreement about comments or ratings? More than likely, the team member would say, "You never told me I was doing anything wrong," or "Why didn't you tell me when I was doing it instead of waiting until now." No one likes surprises when it comes to reviews. If you wait until the review to coach someone, think about the productivity and quality lost throughout the year. Remember that you wanted to be treated fairly and so do your team members. Make sure to treat your team members the same way. If you have coached the team member properly throughout the year, there will not be any surprises at review time.

Reviews, promotions, and merit increases: Plan the review process and work the plan.

Coaching

Managing people is a lot like having kids; sometimes we forget to recognize them. When you have someone doing a good job, praise him or her in public—and praise them often. People love to be told that they are doing well. Another part of coaching is to help them on areas that need improvement. This type of coaching should always be done in private. It is an issue between the team member and his or her supervisor—not the department.

A good leader will make sure to praise someone in front of as many folks as possible. It can be in a common work area, lunchroom, or maybe in the weekly staff meeting. It can be as simple as a verbal recognition in front of their peers or as elaborate as a potluck lunch where you serve people and present a gift certificate, a thank you card, or a plaque.

The bottom line is to praise in public and praise as often as you can. You do not want the people on your team to see you only when things are going wrong. You will hear me mention often to only criticize your people in private. A leader is always prepared for coaching one of his team members. You will never see a leader attack one of his or her folks in the hallway or elevator. They will set up safe locations (a room with a door—not a cube or shared workspace), they will have written down and studied the information to be communicated (with specific goals or expectations), and they will be in a productive frame of mind. A good leader will never go into a coaching session when they are frustrated, angry, or emotional. They will also be aware of the emotional state of the team member they are coaching. Coaching sessions are meant to provide one of two outcomes. Either the team member will be coached up to the level of performance they need to be at—or they will be coached out the door. And, I do mean out the door! A good leader will never unload a bad performer on another manager in the company. It would be very easy to let them apply for another job to get rid of them, but it is not the right thing to do. If you have truly worked hard to turn the employee around and they have failed to make improvements, it is probably best for the team member to move on to the next company. We do not want to dump a problem child on another manager's team. Good leaders will make themselves seen. If you put an appointment on your schedule every week for walking around to speak with people, it can pay big benefits. It takes commitment, but your people will respect you and trust you more when they see that you are serious about it. Only seeing a boss walking around when bad news is in the air establishes bad karma.

Insanity is doing the same thing and expecting different results. If a team member is doing something wrong, is it fair to expect different behavior if you do not tell him or her? No, it is not. A leader must always coach in a timely manner when an event or issue happens. Do not put it off. There is nothing worse than getting to your annual review and being told that you made a mistake six months ago—or that you've been doing something the wrong way for several months. As a coach, you need to present your coaching as a professional. Always treat the other person as you would want to be treated. Coaching requires that you show dignity and respect for both your team member and yourself. Remember that you are a role model. The person you are coaching today could be a coach of tomorrow.

Recognize people often—and make it fun. It does not have to cost a lot. Buy them a coffee or soda or take them to lunch. It can be as simple as a handshake or a mention in the staff or department meeting. Remember to treat them as you want to be treated. Even though an individual is ultimately responsible for his or her own career growth, you, as the coach, play a big part in the process. Through discussions with the team member, you should be able to direct them toward the right path. Many times, team members are looking for help in understanding what options are available to them. Giving them direction or assistance can make it much less stressful for them. If you are not sure, then do some research for them with your peers in the company. You are all on the same team—and most peers are more than willing to share information. Going the extra mile to help your team members will show them that you care. This is one of the things that will set you apart from other coaches that are just going through the motions.

Coaching: Praise in public for an honestly earned compliment for work well done.

Corrective Actions

For those of you in managerial roles, there will come a time when corrective action will undoubtedly be required. Team members cannot make changes to their performance or behavior if you do not make them aware of the issue. You own that responsibility, and you need to document the issue in compliance with your company's HR policy and their directions. When an issue comes up, address it with the team member as soon as possible. It should be no longer than a day or so before you talk to the team member. Sometimes a cool down period is wise—just make sure that no more than a day or two passes before you address the problem with your team member. Document each occurrence for your records. Failure to use this simple plan will severely hinder your ability to perform the next actions—when and if it should become necessary. HR must ensure that each team member is treated fairly. If you get HR involved from the beginning, you will save yourself time and frustration. In the event that you have repeat offenders, a thirty-, sixty—or ninety-day performance plan may be an avenue you want to pursue. When team members negatively affect other members of the team, it will start to affect the team's morale and performance. Remember that one bad banana will spoil the bunch. If you do not deal with it—and quickly—the situation will only get worse. You may have to make an employment decision when you find yourself expending more energy coaching a team member than you are leading the team toward its goals and objectives. You are a role model and they are watching you. You have to drive a stake in the ground to say that if they are not turned around by this date, I must move to the next level. Termination, as unpleasant as it may be, must always be kept as an option for severe performance issues.

I worked for a company in the late 1980s that went through some really tough times; it had eleven downsizings in thirteen years. I was a manager during that time, and I had a tape librarian who had an attendance problem. She was on corrective action when one of the downsizings occurred. Let me make it very clear to everyone that terminating someone is one of the hardest things a manager will ever do. Even if the person deserves it, it will keep you at up nights. You are dealing with people's livelihoods and you never want to take that lightly. I had to cut my headcount by one. All the staff members, except the tape librarian, performed well. She had been an on-again-off-again performer for the past six months. I had serious concerns that she would not be able to turn her performance around, and so she was terminated. During the discussion, she became very emotional and continued to say that she could change. She was thirty days into a ninety-day plan, but she was not showing signs of improvement. I explained to her several times my reasoning for the decision for the termination, but in her emotional state, she could not comprehend. We ended the discussion, and I walked her out.

For the next two weeks, she called daily to try to get her job back. I had referred her to the HR department for any and all conversations after the termination. I had kept HR in the loop on her performance plan and my reasoning for selecting her for the downsizing. There were no questions or repercussions from my decision, and I believe that it was because I had involved HR early on in the process. This was early on in my career, and—even though it was the right thing to do—it was not easy. Leaders never lose compassion for their people.

Corrective Action: People do not read minds—you need to tell them when their behavior needs to change.

Overreaction

Staying in control is something that you should always strive for. Have you ever worked for a type A personality? You were probably on pins and needles all the time. Screaming, hollering, or going out of control will never pay positive dividends. If you cannot control your emotions, how can you control your team or its future? I once worked for a type A personality and the experience showed me how not to act in a pressure situation. All managers are role models and are observed every minute of every day—in and out of the office. This new director was really attempting to win over the customers. As when anyone new comes in, people will attempt to bypass the established processes and go directly to the new boss to get things done. In this case, the customer made up a story about the data center not getting a job processed in time for month-end closing. The customer contacted the new director, and he immediately went off the deep end. He threatened folks in the data center with their jobs if it ever happened again. The problem was that the director never got the facts before he started to berate people. As the facts proved, the end user had failed to approve the online file to allow the job to run using the correct data. When I gave the director the facts about why the job was delayed, he shrugged his shoulders and said, "Just get it processed as soon as possible." He never did apologize to the data center team about his verbal assault. It was then and there that I knew he was my boss, but not my leader. A good leader would have apologized to the team or, even better, never handled the situation that way in the first place. Eight months later, the director moved on to another job. The data center team and most of the IT department had no respect for him because of his lack of maturity and control. Remember that leaders stay in control.

Some tips for staying in control:

Do not overreact every time something happens. If you go crazy every time something goes wrong, people will not want to bring you bad news. What is wrong with that? When things go wrong, you need to learn from them and put processes or procedures in place to minimize or prevent the problem's recurrence. You cannot do that if people are not bringing the problems to you. Get the facts before you start taking action. If you do not have the facts, get them. Do not jump into the fray without getting your facts straight.

Initial responses may be overblown and full of emotions. Do not make the mistake of going off half-cocked. Get the facts, peel back the emotions, and then make decisions. Imagine overreacting to your boss (or in front of your boss) and then finding out that you were wrong. This could result in several less than desirable outcomes. First, you could feel terrible and frustrated. Secondly, if you repeat this behavior, you may give your boss serious concerns about your managerial ability. There will be plenty of time later to get excited, but you may find that a level headed approach will pay better dividends.

Overreaction: Get the facts and discourage emotion appeal during a problem.

Defusing Hostile Customers

At some time in your life, you have probably seen or had to deal with a hostile customer. The best thing you can do is listen, listen, and listen. When someone is emotional about an issue, you cannot be defensive—and do not interrupt them when they are talking. When they run out of breath, there will be a natural pause. You need to reassure them that you are going to do everything you can to help them. You must be honest and sincere. Ask questions to make sure that you have all the facts before you start making promises to fix the issue. As emotions can run very high at times, it may be wise to allow for a cooling-off period. An easy way to work this in is to say that you want to investigate the issue and make sure that you are fixing the right thing (See the Continuous Improvement chapter). Make a commitment to get back to them by a certain hour or a certain day. I like to use the phrase, "Kill 'em with kindness." That means that I am going to do everything that I can to make the issue right for the customer. It is human nature for people not to like everyone. Sometimes people can be mad at the world—or believe that everyone is against them. There is no better feeling than killing them with kindness, and letting them know that you are on their side. Another rule that I like to use for my team members is to never become unprofessional with the customer. If my team member loses his or her cool and argues with a customer, we all lose. Two wrongs do not make a right. When emotions are running high, it may be best for the team member to hand the issue off to a supervisor. As long as the team members conduct themselves professionally, you, as a manager, can stand behind them. When they lose their cool, you really cannot back them up. The business world has changed significantly in the past twenty years. It is no longer acceptable to only provide a quality product. There are so many competitors with the same or better products—what is going to distinguish you from the competition? It is going to be how you service the customers after the sale. Because of my philosophy of building relationships with customers, I have been successful in defusing hostile customers. You have to be open, honest, and sincere when approaching them. If you have a good relationship with your customers, you will know that something has caused this type of behavior. It may be that their boss has just read them the riot act, it may be an issue with a family member, or it could be their car broke down on the way to work. It could be frustration at continual mistakes by their team or yours. Be sure to listen, listen, and listen. Remaining calm, asking questions, and finding answers to correct or prevent reoccurrences should repair any damage to the relationship. Have you ever received late notification of a project that needed your team's assistance, and the person said your boss or the president of the company wants it done? Some people like to use the old name-dropper approach. It is usually because, somewhere along the line, someone has dropped the planning or communications ball. In some cases, I have responded, "Let me call them to find out," and their whole attitude changes. They were bluffing—you caught them—and now they are between a rock and a hard spot. They are all fired up emotionally, and they are attempting to get you to react out of fear. Usually, that is when the truth comes out about a missed requirement that has caused the panic. People whom I support know not to say, "T. J. says he wants it." Instead, I will speak for myself and communicate properly to those folks that need to be in the loop.

Remember that customers are people too. Customers know when someone is blowing smoke in their face, and they know when someone is sincere. If you are not taking their concerns seriously, are interrupting them, or are giving flippant answers, you will only add to the frustration. Leaders take the high road.

Defusing hostile customers: Get the facts and kill 'em with kindness during an emotional time.

You Are a Role Model

You do not have to be a manager to be a role model. You can be a role model for your family, friends, and business associates. People observe other people all day, every day. Ever sit in an airport and watch the people while you are waiting for your flight? It can be an eye-opening experience. Watch how parents correct—or do not correct—their children in public. Do they take the time to talk and correct them, or are they always yelling and threatening the kids? Have you ever heard parents repeatedly threaten a child, but never do anything? They never follow through with their threat—and the kid keeps acting up. It can be a good indication of how they may act at home. I have seen husbands and wives argue and fight in public about the silliest things. Imagine if you are a manager for a team, and they see you fighting in a meeting with a customer or in public with your spouse. Do not think that they will not share that experience with their teammates when they get back to work. In 2002, my wife and I purchased a new Corvette coupe. One weekend, we took the top off and went cruising around the local beach communities on a Sunday afternoon. We were probably thirty miles away from my office that day. When I went to work on Monday, someone mentioned that so-and-so had seen me cruising the beach in the new car with some chick. Luckily for me, that chick was my wife. The point is that people are watching no matter when or where you may be. You have to be a role model seven days a week, twenty-four hours a day.

Just as you praise in public and coach in private in the work setting, it also applies to our personal lives. Praising your kids at home will show them that you are aware of—and are involved in—their lives.

Most people will respect someone who does not ask them to do anything that they would not do themselves. Maybe that means staying late or coming in on weekends to get projects completed. Maybe moving boxes in the office or setting good examples. When team members see that you walk the walk and talk the talk, trust and loyalty can blossom. It is human nature to want to be treated with respect. In personal and professional life, people want to be talked to and not talked at. Whether they are children or adults, you will either win or lose their respect by your actions. When I took over running a company's data center in the mid-eighties I always helped the computer operators move boxes, put tapes back in the tape library, raise floor tiles, and pull cables while wearing my shirt and tie. My team knew that I would help anytime or any place when there was work to be done. This can be in or out of the office environment. While at this company, we would help each other with home projects. When one of our peers needed help, we would put teams together to help on the weekends. I have helped re-roof three houses, install hardwood floors, and helped with countless yard and garage projects. The owner would buy food and drinks for the team, and the job would get done. I showed people that by building strong relationships, anyone on the team could count on me when they needed me. Good role models will give their people their undivided attention. They will be present when meeting with them or talking to them on the phone. They will look them in the eye and pay attention. I have always felt uncomfortable when speaking with people who won't look me in the eye. It may be that they are feeling funny about it, but I always wonder whether I can trust them.

Managing people and being a parent have many similarities. Do you listen to family or company team members when they are talking to you? Do you give them your undivided attention? Most people do not like being ignored—and I am sure that you are no different. How do you react to volatile situations? Do you attack someone in meetings or do you wait to coach them in private? Some of us are continuously under the microscope. You owe it to yourself to stay in control and set positive examples.

You are a role model: Walk the walk and talk the talk rather than saying one thing and doing another.

Reason for a "No" Decision

Ah yes, the word that we started learning when we were six months old. *No* has always been a hard word to accept. It is normal to disagree about opinions or solutions. I have always felt better about being told no when I was told why. It did not change the answer, but knowing the thought process behind the answer allowed me to accept it and move on. Keeping in mind the philosophy of treating people the way you would like to be treated, I have found it well worth taking an extra few minutes to explain the reasons behind the decision. By making the extra effort to explain the reasons, the team is able to see the bigger picture and more able to accept or deal with the answer. There will be times that the answer is confidential and you cannot share the specifics. If you have done a good job of building trust with your team, saying the matter is confidential will be an acceptable answer. Again, you are showing them that you respect their feelings as a team member.

I really believe that a big reason for my success as a leader has been my approach to saying no. Throughout the years, I have always taken the extra time to explain why things were going on. I have been through eleven layoffs at one company, a data center relocation, the consolidation of five help desks, and a relocation of a help desk to a different state. Through all of these events, people wanted—and needed—to receive open and honest communications and be treated with respect.

Taking the time to explain things to them (sometimes multiple times) helped them through some very difficult times in their lives. As I mentioned previously, making sure that people have as much information as possible allows them to make better decisions. When your job is being moved to a different city, and you have to decide to go or stay, it can be terrifying. Good leaders will take as much time as necessary to ensure that their people's questions are answered. This can mean giving up time at lunch, staying late, or rearranging your schedule to accommodate a face-to-face meeting. It may sound like a big burden, but wouldn't you want your leader to do the same for you if you were one of the impacted team members?

Reason for a no decision: When deciding against an action, plan, or request, provide the reason for the decision.

Vendor Management

Both in business and in your personal life, vendor or supplier management can be a challenge. When you look for vendors, make sure that you are looking for those that want to build lasting relationships instead of just selling you something. They need to understand your business or personal needs. They need to be honest about what they can provide. You need to set firm expectations on what your requirements are. An old saying—service after the sale—is even more important today. As the emphasis shifts from products to services, your vendor needs to be on board and be able to support it. Just as when coaching your team members, you need to let the vendors know when they are doing well and when they are not. They cannot correct their service if you do not let them know that you are not happy. As much as they would like us to believe, they are not mind readers. Here comes that role model thing again. If your vendors are not performing, you must put them on notice. You cannot show favoritism to them. Business is business—and if you are not setting a good example for your team, they will never learn to manage vendors. You have to be honest with the vendors and yourself. I am not going to let a vendor perform at a substandard level for my home—why should I let them for my company. Your ability to keep your vendors performing to expectation for a fair price will add to the company's bottom line. That provides opportunities for profit, bonuses, and pay increases. The money has to come from somewhere. Make sure your vendors are earning their money.

In today's economic climate, many companies are out looking to contract, outsource, and even offshore work. With that said, vendor management takes on an even more important role.

We can outsource for a number of reasons:

- Specific skill set not on the current team
- Spike in workload and limited in-house resources
- Save money
- Head count freeze or reduction

No matter what the reason for outsourcing, it is critical that you manage the vendors very closely. It starts with getting very strong requirements:

- Work to be done
- Quantity of work
- Hours of support
- Expected results (set up key measurable metric)
- Required skill set

Depending on what function you require, this should be very specific and written into the contract. Be sure that you also include penalties for not meeting the key measurable in the contract. Next, you will need to set up weekly or monthly meetings to evaluate the performance of the key measurable. You will need to track the results as well as get the vendors to report their performance. If they do not match, then you will need to dig into where the discrepancies are coming from. You also want to assign a specific manager from your team to manage the vendor relationship. This person will be the single point of contact (SPOC) for the vendor and for anyone in your company with issues, questions, or requirements. You will want to work with the company communication team (if you have one) to ensure that all company team members are aware of whom to contact if anything comes up with the vendor. The person designated as the SPOC will meet weekly or monthly to review the performance measurable. These key performance measurements will determine the success or failure of the vendor to perform the services. It will be the SPOC's responsibility to escalate to management in the both companies. You have to hold the SPOC and the vendor accountable for their performance. Without this type of vendor management, the vendors will manage themselves—and the desired results will be in jeopardy.

Vendor management: Be sure to check your vendors' progress and hold them to their commitments.

Passion

We all have different degrees of passion in our personal and professional pursuits. It is about wanting to do the best, be the best, and share life experiences with others. You can tell the ones who love what they do. It may be their smile—or their excitement for doing what they do. There is nothing worse than doing a job you hate. Ever ask someone at the office how they were doing? They said, "I'm here." or "I'm hanging in there." You can tell they are not happy with something. If you are the one responding this way, then this is when you have to look deep inside yourself to determine what makes you happy. If you are not happy doing what you do, it may be time to make some new choices. People pick certain careers because of money, title, or the prestige of the company. If you are not happy, it does not matter how much you make, what your title is, or where you work. Life is short, and many times people will muddle through unhappily. I took a pay cut when our first daughter was born. I went from third shift to first so that I could be home at night with my family. Later, after the birth of our other two daughters, I left a successful job that required significant amounts of travel. My wife and I wanted to be active in their school years, and we could not do that with me on the road all the time. We have never regretted those decisions.

You can have passion no matter what your job is. Recently my wife and I were fortunate enough to go on a baseball spring training road trip in Florida. We live in Florida and love going to spring training games each year. This year, we decided to visit every team field in Florida. On this particular day, we were at the Boston Red

Sox stadium in Ft. Myers. We arrived at 8:30 a.m. for a 1:00 p.m. game to secure tickets. The parking attendants were the only visible employees. After we paid, they pointed us to the guys with the flags directing the cars. As we passed from attendant to attendant, we arrived at the row where they wanted us to park. An older guy with an orange flag signaled us to come forward. I rolled down the window to find that he was talking to us. He yelled at the top of his voice, "Bring it, Chevy. Bring it, Chevy. Right here, Chevy." Then he screamed, "Bam! You're good, Chevy."

He told us to enjoy the game and moved on to the next car being parked. As was our tradition, we tailgated for a couple of hours before going inside the stadium. We pulled out our chairs and cooler and proceeded to hear him direct cars to their spots. I was blown away to hear this guy's enthusiasm as he yelled, "Bring it, Ford. Bring it, Ford. Right here, Ford. Bam! You're good, Ford."

You would have thought this guy was directing traffic on an aircraft carrier. His passion for his job was unbelievable, and it never changed the entire time we sat there. We later found out that he was a volunteer from a local men's club. He was not making a dime, but he chose to create a positive experience for everyone he met that day. That experience will be talked about for years. He made the choice to be positive and spread his positive spirit.

Whether you are a volunteer for a local organization, someone working his or her way to the top of the corporate ladder, or someone in between, you're going to need passion for what you're doing to be successful. The skills we have added to your tool set during our time together can help you improve things for your customers, peers, people you support, and yourself. It is all about people and our ability to get things done correctly, quickly, and to everyone's satisfaction.

What kind of passion do you show in your job?

Passion: Evaluate your own drive and engagement in your profession and enjoy the rewards of your efforts.

Summary

I hope that this book has been beneficial to you and that you will be able to use some of what you have learned in your day-to-day routine.

Part of the reason that I wanted to write this book was to share what I have learned over the years with others. I have seen people struggle to deal with each other every day for the last forty years. As you can see after reading this book, it is not that hard to understand why—if you know what to look for. If I can share my experiences and help others to deal with people easier and more effectively, then I have accomplished my goal. Please do not believe that you have to be in a big company to benefit from this book. Regardless of the industry you work in or the size of your team you can have challenges. Being open and honest with your customers or coworkers should always be a part of your daily life. When making and keeping commitments always remember to treat everyone the way you would like to be treated. The great thing about what I have shared is that it can fit any size organization. Every company can make quality, performance, or organizational improvements—no matter how long it has been in business. I have a strong passion for helping others on this path and am available for speaking engagements as well as private consulting sessions. This is not a perfect world and life can present us with tremendous challenges from time to time. These challenges are not what define us rather it is how we react to these challenges that will distinguish you as a person or as a leader. Your ability to deal positively with these challenges can help you in maintaining balance in your life. The more successful you are in dealing with people and situations can be critical to the future growth and maturation of you and your team. You can delay getting you or your team started on the road to improvements or you can start today. I wish you the best on your journey.